Staff Credits

Editorial: Rona Rosen, Joan Curtis, John Morgan, Marylou McLaughlin

Design: Ken McMullen, Frank Ossman, Gary Blake

Copyright © 1978 by Reverend Francis X. Murphy C.S S.R.

Library of Congress Catalog Card Number 78-66213

Produced by Custombook, Inc., The Custom Building, So. Hackensack, NJ 07606, 883

# CONTENTS

*We gratefully acknowledge*
*the valuable help*
*given by the following people:*

Photo credits:

REVEREND HERBERT DERWERT
REVEREND FRANCIS SKALSKI
MONSIGNOR RAYMOND A. PUNDA
SISTER MARY JUSTITIA
VERY REVEREND STANLEY E. MILEWSKI
REVEREND WILLIAM BURKE
REVEREND WILLIAM BRADLEY
PROFESSOR WACLAW SROKA
MICHAEL KROLEWSKI
WOJCIECH WOJTYSIAK
JUDY SCHIERA

Norman Shaifer
G. Felici
Giancarlo Giuliani
Michael Norcia
Monsignor John P. Foley
Religious News Service
*L'Osservatore Romano*
*The Chicago Catholic*
*The Catholic Standard and Times*
*The Catholic Transcript*
*Polish Daily News*

# FOREWORD

The unexpected deaths of two Popes in a matter of weeks did little to prepare Vatican observers for the surprise election of the first non-Italian Pope in over four centuries! As a Catholic, I was deeply interested in the selection of the successor to Pope John Paul I, whose pontificate was abruptly ended by his untimely death.

However logical the selection of Karol Wojtyla may now seem to some, I had not imagined, as an American Catholic of Polish heritage, that the awesome responsibility to follow in the footsteps of St. Peter would fall to a Polish Cardinal whom I had met first in his own See in Krakow, subsequently on his visit to this country in 1976, and recently as a special representative of the President at his investiture.

Many observers feel that the skills of negotiation demonstrated by Pope John Paul II in his dealings with the Polish government will come into play in developing future relationships between the Vatican and the Communist bloc. This seems like a realistic expectation. But it must be remembered that the Pope's religious dominion is worldwide and his responsibilities and interests are incredibly diverse.

I believe that Pope John Paul II will have a significant impact not only on the Catholic Church but on the entire world. His influence is likely to touch hundreds of millions beyond the membership of the church. An understanding of this humble man of God who, in his own words, came to the Chair of Peter in Rome "...full of trepidation, conscious of his unworthiness," is vital to an understanding of world affairs. Knowing him through the story of his life, from his writings and from the observations of those who have come to know him well, will help us recognize the significance of the events in which the Vatican plays a role as they unfold as a part of contemporary history.

Representative Clement J. Zablocki
Congress of the United States
November 13, 1978

"I announce to you a message of great joy:
We have a Pope."

# 1 KAROL WOJTYLA: THE MAN AND THE PRIEST

The Holy Father, Pope John Paul II, in the first few months of his reign as Bishop of Rome, has already proven himself to be both holy and a father. In his very first address to both the Cardinals in the Sistine Chapel and to all the world, the day after his election, he said he would do two things — help the Church redeem a sense of holiness by putting Vatican Council II into full effect, while at the same time he would reach out to all of mankind to give them a sense of the goodness of God who wants men, women and children to enjoy this world — despite its evils — on their way to eternity.

Just why the Holy Spirit allowed his predecessor, Pope John Paul I, to reign as Pope for only 34 days is a great mystery. But one thing is certain; the man chosen as his successor by the Cardinals representing the whole Church — Cardinal Karol Wojtyla as John Paul II — has already impressed the world with the spirit of joy and hope that the

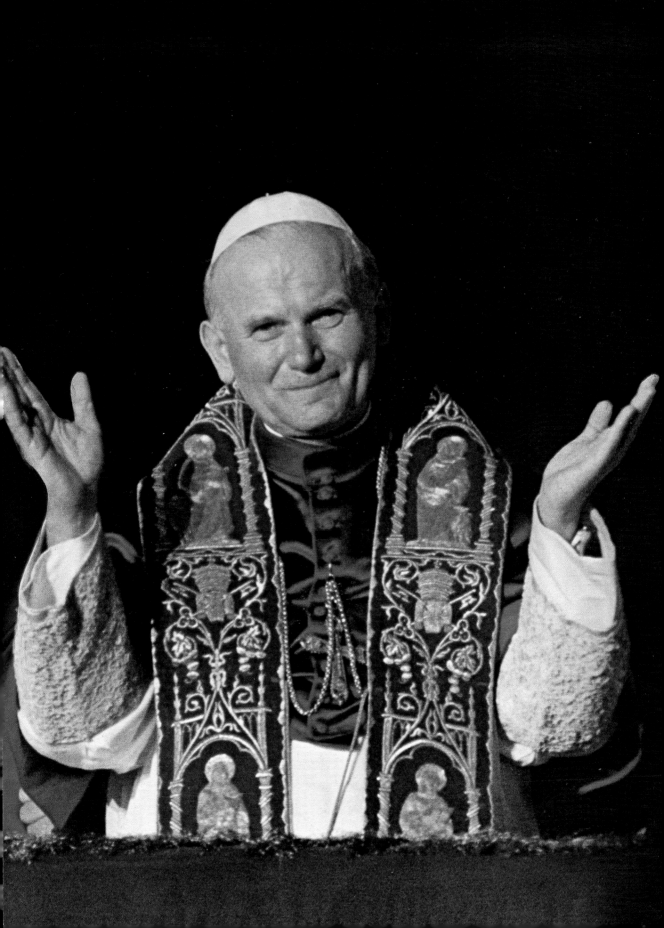

*A family portrait in 1923, when Karol Wojtyla was little more than two years old*

*Dressed in the traditional white suit, the future Pope made his First Holy Communion in 1927*

Cardinal of Venice, as Pope John Paul I, had impressed on the Church.

With his great strength, his wisdom, his knowledge of the world and, above all else, his love for people, great and small, Pope John Paul II has already won the affection of the Church's friends and the respect of its adversaries. Thus he is in a position, and he knows it, to carry out the desires of Pope John XXIII, the plans of Pope Paul VI, and the vision of Pope John Paul I.

Karol Wojtyla was born in the small suburban town of Wadowice outside Krakow on May 18, 1920. A devout Catholic from childhood, he was not cut out for the priesthood from the start. He was educated in the public grammar and high schools of his native town with a heavy emphasis on the classics and the Polish version of European history down to the Nazi invasion of Poland in 1939. His mother died when he was nine, and he was brought up by his father, a retired junior officer in the Polish army. He had a sister who died early in life, and a brother who was killed shortly after becoming a medical doctor.

While in high school Karol had been extremely active in literary and theatrical enterprises connected with both his academic studies and his religious convictions. He supported himself, in part, by working in a nearby stone quarry, and when the war broke out in 1939, he got a full-time job in the Solvay Chemical Works, thus avoiding transportation to Germany as part of a labor gang.

Meanwhile he took an active part in the heroic anti-Nazi resistance movement until he was rescued by Cardinal Sapieha of Krakow. The Cardinal took him and some six or seven other young men into his episcopal residence where they clandestinely studied for the priesthood while quietly aiding the Cardinal in his opposition to the Nazi invaders. Karol Wojtyla also turned a hand to contemporary existentialistic poetry, under the pseudonym of Andrzej Jawien. He wrote a series of sophisticated poems that appeared almost weekly in the *Tygodnik Powszechny — The Weekly Universe —* as a mirror for contemporary men and women suffering from interior anguish about their faith and position in the world.

Originally, he wanted to deal with the problems of the main character in the famous

*Combining his love for the outdoors with his scholarly pursuits, Karol Wojtyla takes time out from rowing his kayak to read — 1955*

*Karol Wojtyla at twenty-five years of age*

novel, *Sky and Flames*, written by the well-known Polish Catholic novelist Tom Boski. The protagonist, Andrzej Jawien, a young, intellectual Catholic gradually losing his faith, was the source of his pseudonym. One of his other works is a social commentary on industrial life dealing with the frustration and despair of a young factory worker's alienation from himself and society. He also wrote phenomenological poetry and about his experience before World War II with the "Rhapsodic Theater" group that went underground during the Nazi occupation but helped uphold the courage and principles of the resistance movement. The following is an example of his sensitive poetry on children:

THE CHILDREN

Love grows within you in its own fashion.
Then, without warning, your elders take you
     by the hand and lead you into the
     vastness of humanity.
(Your hearts are encaged like birds while the
     air around you seems to be all darkness).
I know that in your hearts there beats the
     pulse of mankind.
So taking each other by the hand you sit in
     silence on the riverbank.
A tree trunk against the earth in the light
     of the moon — a triangle in the
     vanishing light.
The fog is not yet risen while the children's
     hearts reach out following the stream.
Will it be ever thus? — I ask — when they
     find their own directions and go off?
Or otherwise. An aureola of light lies among
     these plants and discovers in each a
     depth hitherto unsuspected.
What has begun within you, will you succeed
     in not destroying?
Will you always understand what is right and
     what is wrong?

In the brief interval of peace and rebuilding in Krakow following the cessation of hostilities in 1945, he went to the Krakow seminary where he was ordained a priest on November 1, 1946. He was sent to Rome to do graduate studies in philosophy at the Dominican-run Angelicum — the center of Thomistic theology then enjoying a great renewal as the primary explanation of the Catholic religion. Among his professors was

*A prophetic moment — soon after his elevation to the papacy, Pope John Paul I chats with the Polish Cardinal destined to succeed him in less than two months' time*

the renowned Dominican theologian, the French Father Reginald Garrigou-Lagrange. Upon his arrival in Rome for these post-graduate studies, this large framed, intelligent Polish priest took up residence at the Belgian college and immediately made friends with a number of American as well as other European students. During his studies he developed a special interest in the seventeenth century Spanish mystical writer, St. John of the Cross, whose terribly realistic theology had gotten him into trouble with both the Church and the State. St. John spent some time in prison for his faith. The experience of writing his doctoral dissertation in ethics about St. John of the Cross has imbued Cardinal Wojtyla with a very deep mystical sense in his spiritual life.

Besides absorbing the textbook theology taught in Latin in Rome and engaging in the normal academic arguments common among disputatious clerical students, the energetic priest from Krakow gave spiritual and pastoral assistance to the Polish refugees in Rome and to the innumerable former Polish soldiers and their families who were scattered through Germany, France, and Belgium in the period right after the war. He thus achieved an early acquaintance with much of war-torn Europe and perfected his knowledge of European languages and English. His principal financial support came from the Vatican through the generosity of the United States war relief services under Monsignor Andrew Landi and Mr. James Norris. During this period he was providentially supervised by the substitute Secretary of State, Monsignor Giovanni Battista Montini, the future Pope Paul VI.

Father Karol Wojtyla returned to Poland in 1948, to do parish work and to teach. He also had his first difficult experiences with the pressures of the Communist takeover of his native land. Nevertheless he matriculated at the State University in Krakow in the Theology Department where he took additional courses in moral philosophy, earned a second doctorate, this time in theology, and served as a popular counselor and instructor of students. In 1954, he transferred to the Catholic University of Lublin as Professor of philosophy and ethics. Meanwhile he had not neglected contact with the young university students in the capacity of chaplain and advisor as well as clerical bon-vivant who went

13

Karol Cardinal Wojtyla visited the United States in 1969 and in 1976. Here he blesses parishioners in a parish in Detroit during his second visit and...

...prays at a ceremony in front of a Chicago church. He also toured St. Mary of Nazareth Hospital (upper photo), Chicago, stopping to chat with Helen Zielinski, president of the Polish Women's Alliance

on skiing, canoeing, and camping trips with them and encouraged them in their theatrical, literary, and aesthetic enterprises.

In 1958, at the age of 38, he was made an auxiliary bishop in his native diocese of Krakow. His education in the politics of determined, but non-violent opposition to the persecutionary tactics of the Soviet-controlled Polish Communists was swift and thorough. Nevertheless in 1964, Pope Paul VI managed to have him take over the government of the Archdiocese of Krakow as its new Archbishop.

Immediately after this appointment, the Polish government attempted to profit by the difference between his opposition to its oppressive tactics and those of the hard-hitting, intransigent Cardinal Stefan Wyszynski in Warsaw. But the effort proved futile. In dealing with the Polish authorities Cardinal Wojtyla proved to be smoother, but just as effective as the man of the iron fist — Cardinal Stefan Wyszynski. The two high church prelates and their courageous bishops gradually forced the government to let them build churches and schools needed by the growing Catholic population. They also pressed for the expansion of the rights to publish needed Catholic books and periodicals.

During the pontificates of John XXIII and Paul VI, both prelates became important members of Vatican Council II — Cardinal Wyszynski as one of the board of twelve presidents and Wojtyla as a well-trained theologian involved in the commissions dealing with doctrinal and pastoral problems. Unlike most other prelates from the Communist countries, Wojtyla took a comparatively open progressive stand on these issues, particularly those dealing with marriage, sex, and family life. He likewise showed himself extremely sensitive and open-minded to the issues involved in religious freedom, coming out strongly for the right of the faithful as well as the theologian to discuss the church's teachings freely and to hold differing opinions within the circle of orthodoxy.

Ever since his return to Poland from Rome in 1948, he had supported groups of Catholic intellectuals interested in literature and the arts.

He had been a pillar of strength to the Znak group who, under the guidance of jour-

*Cardinal Wojtyla of Krakow and Stefan Cardinal Wyszynski of Warsaw, fourth from right, were entertained by the American Cardinals on the occasion of the anniversary of the episcopal ordination of John Cardinal Krol of Philadelphia on September 2, 1978, at Villa Stritch, the residence for American clergy working in Rome*

*In 1969, Cardinal Wojtyla visited New Britain, Connecticut. Governor John Dempsey is in the background, left, and Monsignor John Wodarski, pastor of Holy Cross in New Britain, right*

nalist Jerzy Witorowicz, managed to publish a weekly Catholic paper and a monthly periodical called—*Znak-The Sign.* Meanwhile, Wojtyla himself had started to write for publication. He did a study of the German existentialist philosophers. In his book, *Love and Responsibility,* he anticipated both the great advances made in understanding the mutual love of relationships between husband and wife achieved by the pastoral constitution,*Gaudium et Spes,* of Vatican Council II. The sensitivity and realism of this book — a study of sexual morality — led to those foolish and false rumors immediately after his election as Pope that he had been a married man before World War II.

Wojtyla traveled widely at the request of various universities around the world giving technical lectures on modern philosophical problems. He has spoken in Australia and New Zealand as well as in the United States at such universities as Harvard and Princeton.

After attending the Eucharistic Congress in Philadelphia in 1976, he made a wide swing through most of the major Polish Catholic communities and cities in the United States and Canada. He also visited the small, but heavily Catholic nations of Latin America.

Yet despite his duties as Archbishop and his wide travels, Wojtyla always found time to foster and develop his own joyous spirituality.

Four days before the opening of the conclave whence he emerged as John Paul II he made a spiritual retreat high in the Italian mountains east of Rome at a shrine conducted by the Polish-originated Resurrectionist Fathers.

# 2 THE CONCLAVE AND THE VOTING PROCESS

After the death of a Pope, a complex mechanism goes into effect to fill the void at the pinnacle of the Roman Catholic Church. Taking over immediately as the leader of the Church is the Secretary of State who in turn advises the Cardinals of the world of the Pope's death. Upon hearing this news, all the Cardinals throughout the world come to Rome. Soon after the death has occurred, and not more than a few days later, those Cardinals already present in Rome form a committee and begin to make plans for the conclave that will select the new Pope.

Procedures for the entire process, from the moment of the death of the Pope until the conclave begins, have been worked out carefully and have evolved into the way matters are handled at the present time. The mechanism has proven to be valid for the two elections in 1978.

While the discussions begin immediately among the Cardinals as to who might be the most likely candidate to become the successor to St. Peter, the actual deliberations do not commence until the beginning of the conclave.

For the voting, each Cardinal is assigned to a particular place at the tables arranged in the Sistine Chapel. In front of each chair, there is a leather folder, a pen, three ballots, and a large sheet of paper on which to keep track of the votes. The rectangular ballot has the words "I elect as Supreme Pontiff" on the upper part and a dotted line on the lower part. Before the altar, there is a table on which are placed a chalice for the votes, a

*Cheers went up from the throngs in St. Peter's Square as white smoke came from the Sistine Chapel (lower photo). They had been disappointed earlier when black smoke indicated the need for another ballot*

*Floodlights light up St. Peter's Square as thousands await word of the selection of a successor to the throne of St. Peter*

*Among the crowd waiting for the white smoke to billow from the Sistine Chapel was the Archbishop of Mexico City, Cardinal Miguel Dario Miranda y Gomez, whose age excluded him from taking part in the voting. Under a ruling set by Pope Paul VI, prelates over 80 years of age are not allowed to participate in the election of a pope*

large ciborium for re-counting votes, a box used for the votes of absent Cardinals, a large box for ballots from previous voting, and a spool of crimson silk thread to bind the ballots. The papal cassocks, in three different sizes, and the crozier are kept in a small room on the left as one faces the altar. The Master of Ceremonies holds the keys to this room.

The Cardinals vote in both a morning and an afternoon session; two votes are expected at each session unless the first one is successful.

At the appointed hour, the Cardinals gather in the Sistine Chapel and Cardinal Camerlengo intones either "Veni Creator" or another prayer. Then the Cardinal Deacon youngest in seniority takes attendance and draws lots to determine the three Cardinals responsible for counting the ballots, the three responsible for gathering the votes of Cardinal electors who are ill, and another three responsible for reviewing the ballots. After the names are selected, those involved with counting the ballots proceed to the side of the table where the actual balloting is done: two on the left and the third on the right. Now the Master of Ceremonies, the Secretary of the Conclave, and any others responsible for the ceremonies leave the Sistine Chapel for the Sala Regia (the Royal Hall); only the Cardinals remain in the Sistine Chapel. The Cardinal Deacon youngest in seniority closes the Chapel from within and holds the key.

In order of seniority, each Cardinal elector brings his completed ballot to the altar, holding it aloft so that it is clearly visible. At the altar, each Cardinal genuflects, prays briefly, and stands to pronounce his oath. Then he places the ballot on the paten, slides it into the chalice, and returns to his chair.

When the balloting is over, the first counter mixes the ballots in the large chalice, after which the last counter totals the ballots making sure each one is visible to the group; then he transfers it from the chalice to the large ciborium. If the number of ballots does not correspond exactly to the number of voters, the ballots are burned and another voting process begins. However, if everything checks, the first ballot counter opens a ballot, observes the name designated, and passes it to the second counter, who also observes the name, and passes it to the third who reads the name aloud. The ballots are examined; the

*Officials in the procedures for selecting a new head of the Church carry out the roles assigned them*

counters tally the votes under each name and record the information on a specially prepared sheet. If no name receives the two-thirds plus one required for election, the second voting process begins immediately; the same ballot counters, "infirmarians" (those responsible for obtaining the ballots of any Cardinal absent because of illness), and reviewers are retained.

If there has been no election after the second voting session, the Cardinal Deacon youngest in seniority opens the door of the Chapel and calls the Secretary of the Conclave and the Master of Ceremonies. They, along with the counters, burn the ballots along with any other written material. If a Pope is not elected within three days, voting is suspended for at least one day. This allows a period of time for prayer, free discussion among the electors, and a brief spiritual exhortation by the senior Cardinal Deacon (Cardinal Felici). Once again the voting begins, but if, after seven voting sessions, no one has been elected, there is another period

of prayer, discussion, and exhortation by the senior Cardinal Priest (Cardinal Siri). Should there be seven more ballots without a definitive election, another pause for prayer, discussion, and exhortation by the senior Cardinal Bishop (Cardinal Villot) ensues. Following this, the Camerlengo consults with the electors concerning the best method of proceeding. Although two-thirds of the votes plus one are still required for election, if the Cardinal electors unanimously choose to act differently, they can either suggest a "compromise" or a proposal that the requirement for election be an absolute majority plus one or a run-off between the two leading contenders in the last balloting.

When a new Pope has been elected, the least senior Cardinal Deacon (Cardinal Ciappi) opens the door of the Sistine Chapel and invites the Secretary of the Conclave and the Master of Ceremonies to enter. He, in turn, invites the Cardinal Camerlengo and the three Cardinals, each of whom is the senior member of the Cardinal Bishops, Cardinal Priests, and Cardinal Deacons, along with the Secretary of the Conclave and two of the Ceremonialists to come before the newly elected Pope. The Cardinal Camerlengo asks the newly elected: "Do you accept your canonical election as the Supreme Pontiff?" If the response is affirmative, the Camerlengo asks: "What name do you choose?" The Master of Ceremonies, acting as a Protonotary Apostolic, draws up the formal document, reads it and co-signs it with the Secretary of the Conclave and two Ceremonialists who act as witnesses.

The Cardinals who are the head of each of the orders of Cardinals, and the Camerlengo return to their places. The Master of Ceremonies leads the newly elected Pontiff to the room in which the papal vestments have been prepared. In the Sistine Chapel, the papal throne has now been set in front of the altar. The new Pope returns to the Chapel and extends his blessing to the Cardinals, who, in turn, come before him, greeting and embracing him in their first act of obedience. The Cardinal Camerlengo places the "fisherman's ring" on the Holy Father's finger; later the Pope will return the ring to the Master of Ceremonies to have his name inscribed. This part of the ceremonies concludes with the Camerlengo intoning the "Te Deum."

# 3 THE ELECTION OF POPE JOHN PAUL II

For the second time in less than two months the world awaited word from the Sistine Chapel about the election of a new Pope. When John Paul I was chosen it took the world by surprise because the decision was made so quickly. At the time, most Romans were on vacation and this late August Saturday almost seemed to disrupt the journalists who were prepared to spend a leisurely weekend, expecting results sometime in the early part of the following week. Because of the speed with which John Paul I was elected, the public, as well as the press, was ready for the same speed this time. At the end of the first day of voting, the square was crowded with Romans and newsmen, expecting an immediate repetition of the white smoke that resulted in the election of John Paul I. But the crowd was disappointed; the conclave did not yield a new Pope at the end of the first day. On the second day of voting, the crowds began to gather in late morning,

waiting for the smoke from the Sistine Chapel, and, as many expected, the result was black smoke.

In the late afternoon, people began to fill the square, watching the chimney for indications of the afternoon deliberations. By this time the Romans and the visitors were becoming accustomed to the twice a day ritual of checking for the smoke; in fact, they arranged their business and sightseeing around the ballot-burning schedule. By the evening of the second day, the atmosphere was charged with tension and the news commentators and Vatican radio broadcasters who could see the smoke stack from their perch on top of the colonnades above the square, began to sense an atmosphere of activity behind the walls of the Vatican. Open windows revealed an inordinate amount of movement in the Papal apartments clearly visible with the aid of binoculars from the vantage point of the colonnades or the piazza. As the tension grew, the experienced observers felt an announcement was in the making and, within a few minutes, the smoke appeared from the Sistine Chapel chimney, first black and then, a few seconds later, white. Radio commentators, on top of the colonnades in plain view of the chimney, contacted their stations as they heard the roar of the crowd at the realization of the election. At that moment, commentators from all parts of the world, pre-empted programs so that they could speak live from St. Peter's. Now the crowd was yelling, jumping, cheering, and, as near pandemonium broke loose, the radio broadcasters obtained the right of way over their air channels and, with great emotion, relayed the news that, "the smoke coming from the chimney of the Sistine Chapel is white. We have a new Pope...we have a new Pope."

Within minutes, people appeared on the top floors of the Borgia Palace as the crowd turned and looked to the balcony in the center of the facade of St. Peter's where they knew the Pope would appear momentarily. As is traditional, the Senior Cardinal Deacon, preceded by the cross bearer and accompanied by two other Cardinals, came out onto the balcony and announced to the world that a new Pope had been chosen, but did not give his name. After this long-awaited-for announcement, several groups of men in colorful uniforms, including a contingent of the

CITTA' DEL VATICANO, LUNEDI' 16 OTTOBRE 1978 · UNA COPIA L. 200

EDIZIONE STRAORDINARIA ORE 18,43

# L'OSSERVATORE ROMANO

### GIORNALE QUOTIDIANO  POLITICO RELIGIOSO

UNICUIQUE SUUM     NON PRAEVALEBUNT

## Habemus Papam

# CAROLUM WOJTYLA

### qui sibi nomen imposuit

# IOANNEM PAULUM II

## *Pietro e padre*

Ti è stato assegnato il mandato così come per la prima volta, in un'alba di venti secoli fa sulla riva del lago di Tiberiade, è stato voluto per Simone, figlio di Giovanni, e da Cristo chiamato « roccia ». Secondo la promessa — « Non vi lascerò orfani » — si è ripetuto l'evento che appartiene al mistero di salvezza della Chiesa e che scandisce il suo cammino nel mondo.

Sei in mezzo a noi il capo visibile della Chiesa della quale Cristo è il capo invisibile: sei con noi, popolo di Dio, e con tutti gli uomini; conosciamo il tuo volto ove, da questo momento, scorgeremo sempre il segno della tua sollecitudine di Supremo Pastore: la tua presenza viene a confermarci la certezza di una continuità e di una comunione che giungeranno a toccare, nella fine dei tempi, la soglia dell'eterno.

Il tuo consenso ai Padri che ti hanno designato nel Conclave, alla luce invocata dallo Spirito che dà la vita, è la risposta trepida e coraggiosa al volere di Dio ed è motivo per rendergli grazie nella gioia del dono che ci ha fatto. Il tuo sì è, per noi credenti e per quanti avvertono l'insostituibile valore della Chiesa nella storia aperta o segreta degli uomini, un tangibile rinnovarsi di speranze.

Ti diciamo la nostra gratitudine per aver assunto il peso enorme del mandato, e ti chiamiamo padre maestro e fratello: è gratitudine che, pur nell'empito festoso del cuore, viene dal profondo dell'animo, nella consapevolezza che la tua è una paternità spirituale nel sacrificio del servizio.

Vieni a confortarci nella fede perché, come in ogni tempo — ma forse più drammaticamente nel nostro —, il « principe di questo mondo » continua a vagliarci. A te, Pietro, è stato dato il potere per mantenere intatto il patrimonio di fede, ma anche per stimolarci a capirne sempre più la portata, perché possiamo essere testimoni sempre più liberi dell'amore di Dio. Siamo, infatti, sempre troppo in spareggio con quello che Cristo ci ha comandato per essere suoi seguaci: non abbiamo gli occhi così limpidi per discernere appieno nei segni dei tempi quanto, oltre la scorza, è più necessario o più vero; né la volontà così pronta per viverlo come è necessario.

Tu vieni per farci da guida in questo cammino perché possiamo essere portatori, nella tormentata storia comune, nella cultura e nella civiltà, nella società e nei doveri quotidiani, di quel sale che non deve insipidire e di quel lievito che non deve indurire.

Tu vieni a ricordarci che la nostra fede non possiamo tenerla al servizio della nostra consolazione privata e ad ammonirci di non essere timorosi nel nostro dissentire dall'orizzontalismo mondano. La tua presenza è una paternità universale; tu sei un punto di riferimento per tutti gli uomini che credono nei valori dello spirito, della pace e della concordia fra i popoli.

Per questo, nel tuo mandato e nel tuo stesso umano sentire si rifletterà la sofferenza dell'amore; la tua risposta alla chiamata è davvero un perdere la vita nel modo più puro e più duro secondo il Vangelo. Tu ami tutti, ma non tutti ti ricambieranno, perché la condizione dei figli è quella di essere manchevoli rispetto a quanto chiedono e a quanto ricevono dalla pienezza del padre. Ed anche in noi credenti, nonostante il volere, la rispondenza non sarà pari alla tua premura, e ciò sarà parte della tua fatica quotidiana e della tua solitudine davanti a Dio: il cammino che hai iniziato è somigliante alla via della croce e nel tuo Primato c'è la corona di spine. Ed anche in questo vediamo la realtà della tua successione a Pietro ed il tuo essere vicario di Cristo.

Per tutto ciò, viva è la nostra gratitudine e profonda la nostra commozione in questa nuova alba, ove così sensibilmente si manifestano l'antica promessa e l'unione ecclesiale, tanto che, nei giorni a venire, non vorremmo disperderne neppure una briciola: lo faremo unendoci a Cristo che prega per te, e con te, che ami la Chiesa e le genti, e ci aiuti ad essere seminatori e testimoni della parola e della carità che non si consumano.

v. v.

Pope's own Swiss Guards marched in formation into the Square; each group had with it a small brass band. More suspenseful minutes...and finally, coming onto the balcony was the new Pope, flanked by the Papal Masters of Ceremonies. When his name was announced by Cardinal Pericle Felici, the crowd reacted with excitement yet surprise because the choice was a non-Italian.

The typical reaction of: "Oh, a foreigner," was short-lived when Cardinal Wojtyla gave the following brief address in flawless Italian to the cheering crowd:

"May Jesus Christ be praised. Dearest brothers and sisters, we are all still grieved after the death of our most beloved Pope John Paul I. And now the most eminent Cardinals have called a new Bishop of Rome. They have called him from a distant country, distant but always so close through the communion in the Christian faith and tradition. I was afraid to accept this nomination but I did it in the spirit of obedience to Our Lord Jesus Christ and of total confidence in his Mother, the most holy Madonna.

"I do not know whether I can explain myself well in your...our Italian language. If I make a mistake you will correct me. And so I present myself to you all to confess our common faith, our hope, our confidence in the Mother of Christ and of the Church, and also to start anew on this road of history and of the Church, with the help of God and with the help of men."

The new Pope then imparted his first Apostolic Blessing, "Urbi et Orbi" (a blessing for the city and the world).

Within about twenty minutes of this emotional speech, an issue of L'Osservatore Romano appeared complete with the picture and a biography of the new Pope. The newspaper had information about all of the Cardinals already set in type; it was just a matter of waiting to learn the name of the winner and rushing it to the presses.

The press knew very little about Cardinal Wojtyla, and there was much scurrying around for background information for the reporters to transmit. A book, published some months before, entitled *The Inner Elite: Dossiers of Papal Candidates* by Gary McEoin, seemed to be in front of every radio and television commentator who was hurriedly reading the one-and-a-half pages about Cardinal Wojtyla. This book gave biographical data on all of the Cardinals who were considered as Papal candidates.

During the first few hours after the election, this information was the primary source for everyone. The same book, used a month-and-a-half earlier when Cardinal Albino Luciani was chosen, was sold out soon after Paul VI died. There was not enough time to reprint it when the election process began that picked Cardinal Wojtyla.

The Polish churchmen in Poland and America were caught off-guard, but the ultimate realization of a Polish Pope resulted in unbounded joy.

Most Polish Americans recalled the visits of Cardinal Wojtyla to America in 1969 as a representative of the Polish Primate, Cardinal Stefan Wyszynski, and in 1976, as a representative to the Eucharistic Congress. He made the rounds of many Polish parishes throughout America and was not considered a stranger anywhere. After the initial excitement, Polish people everywhere wanted to make their way to Rome to view the installation. There was great concern about those in Poland since the government required its residents to have an exit visa. However, there seemed to be so much pressure on the Polish government, that visas were granted almost immediately to thousands who were involved or interested in being present in Rome during the installation. The church people, the news media, friends, family, and many others were permitted to travel from Poland. Only a few, those deemed bona fide risks by the communist government, could not get visas to get to Rome. Between the election and the installation, each day brought more plane loads of Polish people from Poland and America. During this time, the world was beginning to learn more about John Paul II and what could be expected of him was implicit in his Message to the World, to the Cardinals, to the Diplomatic Corps, and to the Press. Enthusiasm for him began to build as he was viewed as a Pope who would be a positive force in the church. The choice of the name, John Paul II, clearly indicated his interest in continuing the pastoral intent of John Paul I. In addition, the new Pope's knowledge of diplomacy, theology, and world matters gave him strengths and advantages where perhaps John Paul I was somewhat less informed.

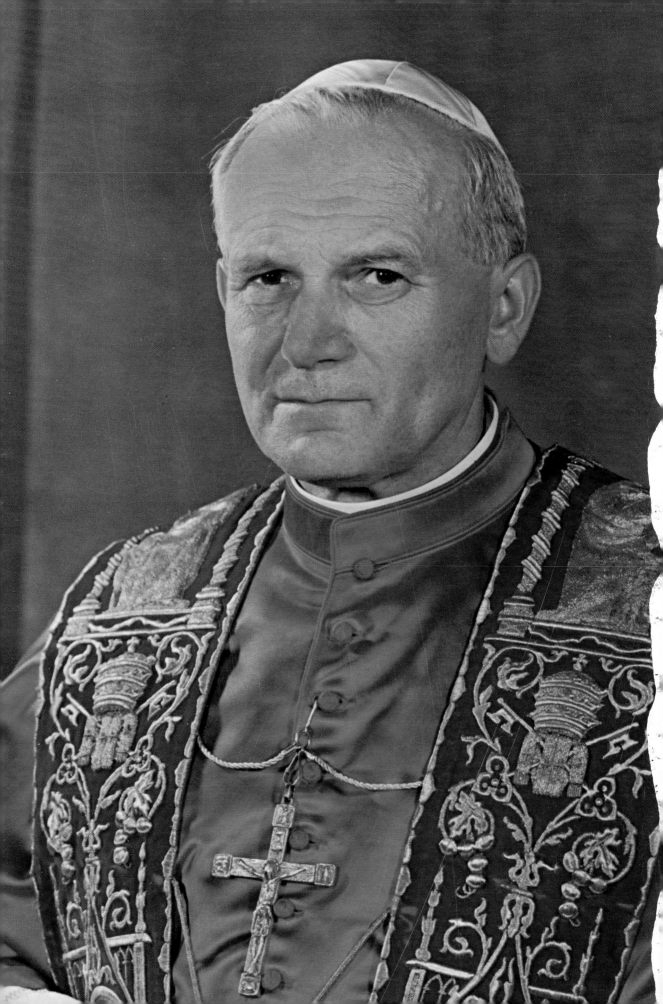

*Pope John Paul II prays at the tomb of his predecessor, whose name he took for his own papacy*

# 4

# JOHN PAUL II's INVESTITURE

After the election, John Paul II decided that he wanted to continue the new trend of holding the installation service outdoors. The day before the Pope's investiture, the barricades and platforms were in the process of being set up on the steps of St. Peter's for the fourth time in three months. The work crew continued through Saturday night in preparation for the 10 a.m. Sunday service which would herald the new ministry.

Starting at 6 a.m. Sunday morning, the long, wide street leading from the Tiber River to St. Peter's was filled with throngs of people who had walked across the bridge to the Vatican. Beginning on Thursday, plane loads of people arrived from Poland and the United States; all wanting to witness the milestone event, the installation of the first non-Italian Pope in 455 years. Because there were many tourists in Rome at this time and a goodly number of Italians who had been on vacation away from the city during John Paul I's installation were now home, the combination of visitors and natives created a festive atmosphere.

Everywhere there were people walking to St. Peter's; the main route was closed to all cars but those VIPS - Kings, Queens, Presidents, and other dignitaries who arrived in heavily guarded motorcades. The great square was filled with thousands of people who stood waiting to view the new leader of the Roman Catholic Church. The security measures around St. Peter's were impressive. They required the coordination of the Italian police, the Vatican police, and the special security guards of each of the heads of State. While the United States Secret Service was not in such force as it was during the inauguration of John Paul I, because of the presence of Vice-President Mondale, it was nevertheless visibly protecting the following United States Presidential delegation: The Honorable and Mrs. Thomas P. O'Neill, Jr., The Honorable Zbigniew Brzezinski, Senator Edmund Muskie, The Honorable Robert F. Wagner, Mr. Peter Sarros, Mrs. Patrick J. Nugent, The Reverend Stanley E. Milewski. The Contingency from Poland was very apparent, showing great curiosity and enthusiasm throughout the impressive ceremony. Limousines, with police escorts, began to arrive before 9 o'clock carrying royalty dressed in full regalia, diplomats wearing brightly colored insignia, and bishops from all over the world who had been staying in Rome most of the previous week.

A group of Americans from Clark's Green, Pennsylvania were among those watching the installation; needless to say they thought themselves some of the luckiest people there. Last spring, the clergy and parishioners of St. Gergory's Church agreed to a pilgrimage to Rome. The trip's arrival and departure dates were fixed many months in advance. These fortunate Americans not only saw Rome, but were privileged to share the jubilation of the installation ceremonies before they returned home the next morning.

Nearly all was ready and everyone was in place before 9:30. For at least an hour before the ceremony, the diplomatic corps caused a huge traffic jam extending across the Tiber; a seemingly endless number of Mercedes limousines lined up as far as the eye could see.

Tickets for the seats at the ceremony were difficult to get. During the days prior to the installation, anyone who had a cousin, uncle, or friend who was either a bishop or connected with the Vatican in any way was bombarded with requests for the special tickets entitling the spectator to a seat in the special up front section. Flanking both sides of the ceremony area were stands facing the

*The many dignitaries and diplomats in Rome for the installation of the new Pope required extensive security precautions (upper photo). Media representatives from around the world were stationed in the Museum of Contemporary Arts*

*The Vatican's Swiss guards were easily recognizable in their distinctive and colorful uniforms*

*Czestochowa, the home of the venerated icon known as "The Black Madonna," was well represented at ceremonies installing a Polish cardinal as the new Vicar of Christ*

*Within days of his ascendancy to the papacy, Pope John Paul II made an unannounced public visit to a hospital in Rome.*

*At 6 p.m. on August 26th, crowds in St. Peter's Square kept their eyes on the chimney above the Sistine Chapel waiting for white smoke to appear (right)*

*The news that a pope had been selected quickly spread throughout Rome and the enormous Square was soon filled by thousands of people hoping to get a view of the new head of the Roman Catholic Church*

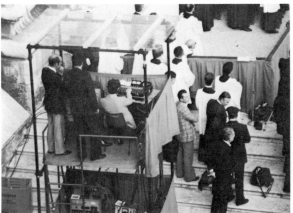

*Media crews positioned themselves in the square and on top of the colonnades*

center; the clergy was on one side and the diplomatic corps was on the other. Facing St. Peter's were the remaining seats, which had been divided into sections and color coded. The festive aura was intensified by the decorative Papal flags hanging from the second story of every building and hotel.

The Renaissance buildings still in use, the ancient church rituals repeated, the colorful clerical garb, the brightly striped costumes and plumed helmets of the Swiss Guard, and the folk costumes of the Italian and Polish villagers, all contributed to the great drama of the scene enacted at the Vatican on the occasion of the Pope's installation. All of this is juxtaposed against the twentieth century so clearly illustrated by the throngs of international journalists equipped with tape recorders and long lenses to cover the event.

In fact, while all the spectators and dignitaries were getting settled, the media had been scurrying to complete their set-up so that broadcasting, television, and films could make it possible for the millions throughout the world who could not be present in person to participate through the mass communications system. The Museum of Contemporary Art in the Vatican, located under the colonnades was cleared out so that television and radio people could set up their equipment to transmit throughout the world. This huge museum had thousands of wires running to hastily set-up control centers, each of which had microphones, telephones, and television editing equipment crammed into very tight spaces. All the major American networks were present. Now there was a full compliment of photographers and radio and television people from Poland who had been meagerly represented at the previous investiture of John Paul I and the election a week earlier.

Promptly at 10 the beautiful ceremony began. It was estimated that over seven hundred million people were watching or listening to the installation from all over the world.

From atop the colonnades, photographers' complex telephoto lenses were trained on the participants in the ceremony so that it was possible, from this vantage point to be as close as if one were only five feet from the celebrants..

The rituals proceeded smoothly and flawlessly.

*The new Pope holds up the host during the Offertory of the Mass celebrated in St. Peter's Square following investiture*

# Celebration for the Beginning of the Ministry

*Everything is prepared at the altar of the Confession of St. Peter in the Basilica as for the blessing of the Pallium on the 28th of June. The Cardinal concelebrants vest in the chapel of St. Sebastian. They then line up for the procession near the chapel of the Blessed Sacrament in the central nave of the Basilica as they await the arrival of the Holy Father. He will arrive from the door of St. Martha (on the left as one faces towards the Bernini Columns) and go down to the tomb of St. Peter to pray. Meanwhile the papal choir sings the hymn "Veni, Creator Spiritus":*

Come, Spirit Creator, come, live in our minds and fill with perfect grace the hearts which you have made.

We know you as the Strengthener, the Gift of God most high, our fire, our love, the living fountain and holy anointing of our lives.

With seven gifts you act as if the finger of the Father's hand, his promised One, to teach us speech and understanding.

Blaze as light within our senses, pour love into our hearts and bring your strength to raise the weakness of our bodies.

Drive Satan far from us and give us lasting peace that, led forward by you, no harm may come to us.

Let us know the Father, through you. Let us know the Son, through you. Let us believe for ever that you are the Spirit proceeding from the Father and the Son. Amen.

*At the end of this hymn the procession prepares to move towards the square. Meanwhile the choir sings a litany of praise alternating with the assembly.*

SCHOLA **(S).**            *RESPONSE (R.)*

**(S.)**    **Hear us O Christ.**
*(R.)*    *Hear us O Christ.*
**(S.)**    **Grant life to John Paul who has been chosen by God as Supreme and Universal Pontiff.**
*(R.)*    *Repeat.*
**(S.)**    **Saviour of the world.**
*(R.)*    *Assist him. (Repeat 3 times.)*
**(S.)**    **Holy Mary.**
*(R.)*    *Assist him.*
**(S.)**    **Holy Mother of the Church.**
*(R.)*    *Assist him. (Repeated after each name.)*
**(S.)**    **St. Michael, St. Gabriel, St. Raphael, St. John the Baptist, St. Joseph, St. Peter, St. Paul, St. Andrew, St. James, St. John, St. Thomas, St. James, St. Philip, St. Bartholomew, St. Matthew, St. Simon, St. Thaddeus, St. Mathius, St. Barnabas, St. Luke, St. Mark, St. Stephen, St. Leo, St. Gregory, St. Basil, St. Benedict, St. Dominic, St. Francis, St. Agnes, St. Cecilia, St. Lucy.**
**(S.)**    **Lord have mercy.**
*(R.)*    *Lord have mercy.*
**(S.)**    **Christ have mercy.**

*Hundreds of clergy holding chalices full of hosts await the moment to distribute Communion to the crowds*

*(R.)*     *Christ have mercy.*

**All:**     **Lord have mercy.**

*The procession enters through the central door and exits into the Piazza by a side door. The ceremonialists, the four deacons of the Roman rite, the assistant deacon and the deacon of the Greek rite approach the altar and put the Gospel book in its proper place. A deacon carries the Pallium on a tray. The Cardinals come before the altar and reverence the altar. They then go to their places.*

*The Holy Father arrives at the altar and bows to it, wearing the mitre and carrying the pastoral cross. The Pope then goes in front of the altar to greet the assembly. He returns to the altar, the mitre is removed and the pastoral cross given to an assistant. He kisses the altar with an assisting deacon, incenses the altar. Receiving the mitre and pastoral cross, he goes to his chair before the central door of St. Peter's.*

*He sits on the chair for a few moments wearing his mitre and holding his cross. He then stands and chants:*

**In the name of the Father and of the Son and of the Holy Spirit.**

*(R.)*     *Amen.*

**Peace be with you.**

*(R.)*     *And with your spirit.*

*The Pope is again seated. The Cardinal proto-deacon (Cardinal Pericle Felici) goes to the altar, takes the tray with the Pallium and comes before the Holy Father to place the Pallium upon him. He says the following prayer:*

**Blessed be God who has chosen you to be Pastor of the Universal Church, and who has clothed you with the shining stole of your apostolate. May you reign gloriously** here on earth for long years, until when called by your Lord you will possess the stole of immortality in the kingdom of heaven. Amen.

*The mitre is then placed on the head of the Holy Father. The Cardinals come one after another, genuflect before him, kiss his hand as a sign of obedience and receive the kiss of peace. Meanwhile the choir and congregation sing the antiphon:*

*You are Peter and upon this rock I will build my Church.*

*They alternate this Antiphon with the Canticle:* **Blessed be God, the Father of Our Lord Jesus Christ (Ephesians 1, 3-10).**

**(S.)**     **Blessed be God the Father of Our Lord Jesus Christ who has blessed us with all the spiritual blessings of heaven in Christ.**

*(R.)*     *Antiphon.*

**(S.)**     **Before the world was made, he chose us, in Christ to be holy and spotless and to live through love in his presence.**

*(R.)*     *Antiphon.*

**(S.)**     **He determined that we should become his adopted sons through Jesus Christ for his own purposes.**

*(R.)*     *Antiphon.*

**(S.)**     **To make us praise the glory of his grace, his free gift to us in the Beloved.**

*(R.)*     *Antiphon.*

**(S.)**     **In whom, through his blood we gain our freedom, the forgiveness of our sins.**

*(R.)*     *Antiphon.*

**(S.)**     **Such is the richness of the grace which he has showed on us in all wisdom and insight.**

*(R.)*     *Antiphon.*

(S.)     He has let us know the mystery of his purpose.

(R.)     *Antiphon.*

(S.)     The hidden plan he so kindly made in Christ from the beginning to act upon when the times had run their course to the end.

(R.)     *Antiphon.*

(S.)     That he would bring everything together under Christ, as Head, everything in the heavens and everything on earth.

(R.)     *Antiphon*

*When this part of the ceremony is completed, the Holy Father will intone the Gloria.*

Glory to the God in the highest, and peace to his people on earth. Lord God, heavenly King, almightly God and Father, we worship you, we give you thanks, we praise you for your glory. Lord Jesus Christ, only Son of the Father, Lord God, Lamb of God, you take away the sin of the world: have mercy on us; you are seated at the right hand of the Father; receive our prayer. For you alone are the Holy One, you alone are the Lord, you alone are the Most High, Jesus Christ, with the Holy Spirit, in the glory of God the Father. Amen.

*The Holy Father then sings:*

Let us pray: O God, who in the plan of your providence has willed to build your Church upon blessed Peter, head of the Apostolic College, look kindly on (me) your Servant. Grant that I whom you have appointed as a successor of Peter, might be the visible source and foundation of the unity of faith and the bond of love. Through our Lord Jesus Christ, your Son, who lives and reigns with you in the unity of the Holy Spirit, one God forever and ever. Amen.

## LITURGY OF THE WORD

*The first reading is in English, the responsorial psalm is in Latin, the second reading is in Polish. Reading number 1: A reading from the book of the Prophet Isaiah (52, 7-10):*

How beautiful on the mountains, are the feet of one who brings good news, who heralds peace, brings happiness, proclaims salvation, and tells Zion, "Your God is king!"

Listen! Your watchmen raise their voices, they shout for joy together, for they see the Lord face to face, as he returns to Zion.

Bring into shouts of joy together, you ruins of Jerusalem; for the Lord is consoling his people, redeeming Jerusalem. The Lord bares his holy arm in the sight of all the nations, and all the ends of the earth shall see the salvation of our God.

(R.)     *Thanks be to God.*
      *Psalm response: (Psalm 44, 116):*

(S.)     You have made them princes.

(R.)     *Over all the earth.*

(S.)     Nations will sing your praises forever.

(R.)     *Over all the earth.*

(S.)     Praise Yahweh, all the nations, extol him all you peoples.

(R.)     *Over all the earth.*

(S.)     For his love is strong, his faithfulness eternal.

(R.)     *Over all the earth.*

*Second Reading: A reading from the first letter of St. Peter (5, 1-4):*

Now I have something to tell your elders: I am an elder myself, and a witness to the sufferings of Christ, and with you I have a share in the glory that is to be revealed. Be the shepherds of the flock of God that is entrusted to you: watch over it, not simply as a duty but gladly, because God wants it; not for sordid money, but because you are eager to do it. Never be a dictator over any group that is put in your charge, but be an example that the whole flock can follow. When the chief shepherd appears, you will be given the crown of unfading glory.

This is the word of the Lord.

(R.)     *Thanks be to God.*

*The Gospel is proclaimed in Latin and in Greek. The Gospel acclamation: Alleluia,*

*alleluia, alleluia.*
(R.)    *Repeated*
(S.)    Jesus said to Simon Peter: "Simon, son of John, do you love me?"
(R.)    *Alleluia.*
(S.)    Peter answered him: "Lord, you know all things, you know that I love you."
(R.)    *Alleluia.*
(S.)    Jesus said to him, "Feed my lambs."
(S.)    The Lord be with you.
(R.)    *And with your spirit.*

A reading from the Holy Gospel according to John (21, 15-17):

After the meal Jesus said to Simon Peter, 'Simon son of John, do you love me more than these others do?' He answered, 'Yes Lord, you know I love you.' Jesus said to him, 'Feed my lambs.' A second time he said to him, 'Simon son of John, do you love me?' He replied, 'Yes, Lord, you know I love you.' Jesus said to him, 'Look after my sheep.' Then he said to him a third time, 'Simon son of John, do you love me?' Peter was upset that he asked him the third time, 'Do you love me?' and said, 'Lord, you know everthing; you know I lovee you.' Jesus said to him, 'Feed my sheep.'

This is the word of the Lord.
(R.)    *Praise to you, O Christ.*

*The Greek deacon then proclaims the same Gospel passage in Greek. The deacon says with loud voice:* **Wisdom! Stand! Let us listen to the Holy Gospel.**

*The Holy Father giving his blessing says:* **Peace to all of you.**
(R.)    *And with your spirit.*

*When the Gospel proclamation is ended, the Choir sings:* **Glory to you O Lord; Glory to you.**

*The deacon hands the Gospel book to the Holy Father. The Holy Father blesses the deacon and with the Gospel book blesses the people, tracing the sign of the cross as he says:* **Peace to you who have announced the Good News.**

*The Holy Father then gives the homily.*

*At the conclusion of the homily the creed will be sung:*

**We believe in one God, the Father, the Almighty, maker of heaven and earth, of all that is seen and unseen.**

**We believe in one Lord, Jesus Christ, the only Son of God, eternally begotten of the Father, God from God, Light from Light, true God from true God, begotten, not made, one in Being with the Father.**

**Through him all things were made. For us men and for our salvation he came down from heaven: by the power of the Holy Spirit he was born of the Virgin Mary, and became man. For our sake he was crucified under Pontius Pilate; he suffered, died, and was buried. On the third day he rose again in fulfillment of the Scriptures; he ascended into heaven and is seated at the right hand of the Father.**

**He will come again in glory to judge the living and the dead, and his kingdom will have no end.**

**We believe in the Holy Spirit the Lord, the giver of life, who proceeds from the Father and the Son. With the Father and the Son he is worshipped and glorified.**

**He has spoken through the Prophets. We believe in one holy catholic and apostolic Church. We acknowledge one baptism for the forgiveness of sins. We look for the resurrection of the dead, and the life of the world to come. Amen.**

*The prayers of the faithful are then chanted by four ministers who will present the intentions in Polish, French, Spanish, English and German.*

---

## GENERAL INTERCESSIONS

*The Holy Father:*

**Brothers, most dear sons and daughters: in this day of joy let us be guided by the Holy Spirit who directs the life of the Church and inspires our prayer. Together we ask our Father who is in heaven for that which we need to live as authentic disciples of Jesus Christ for the glory of God and for the good of all men.**

*The Cantor:*

1.    *For the Holy Church of God, the universal sacrament of salvation, that in the unity desired by Christ, it will always remain faithful to the divine will and announce the Gospel to all men without ceasing.*

2.    *For our Holy Father John Paul, guide for the people of God, that,*

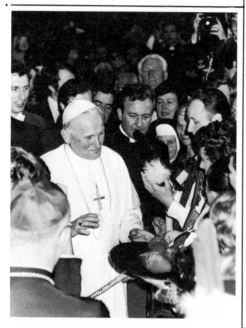

*Pope John Paul II, better known as Cardinal Wojtyla to this proud and happy group of countrymen, takes time to bless loaves of Polish bread (upper photo). The day before his installation, the Pope answered questions and made comments at a press conference*

SANTA MESSA CELEBRATA DAL PAPA GIOVANNI PAOLO II
PER L'INIZIO DEL SUO MINISTERO DI SUPREMO PASTORE

*Cover of the souvenir booklet containing the liturgy for the Mass celebrated by the newly installed pope*

*strong in charity in imitation of the Supreme Pastor, he might strengthen in faith those who live with the hope of eternal life.*

3. *For all men called to live in true brotherhood so that, with the strength of all and in the light of the Gospel, it may be possible to create a new world in justice and in peace.*

4. *For all those who are suffering from war, sickness, hunger or persecution, that the Lord, through the unceasing prayer of the Church may relieve their suffering and turn all sadness into joy.*

5. *For all of us here present, united with our Father in a common faith, that, under his guidance we may be disposed to truly working together to bring to reality the message of the Gospel.*

*The Holy Father concludes:*

**O, God, who disposes with strength and gentleness the days of man and the seasons of life, and who has placed me in the holy Church as servant of your servants, deign to accept this our prayer and unite into a single heart, the people and their Priest, so that there will always be docility to the Shepherd by the faithful and the care of the Shepherd for the faithful.**

## LITURGY OF THE EUCHARIST

*The Offertory Procession takes place. Various ministers will bring the paten with the host to the Hoy Father, the cruets with wine and water, the ciborium for communion that will be used by the Pope (also two bouquets of flowers and two candles). Other items are brought to the two deacons who will prepare the altar. When the preparations are completed the Pope will approach the altar with two assistant deacons and other ministers. After offering the bread and wine he will incense the altar. Then he in turn is incensed by the Deacon.*

*The washing of hands will take place after the incensation. During this part of the liturgy the choir and congregation sing the offertory canticle:*

*Antiphon: The Spirit of the Lord is upon me. He has sent me to bring the good news to the poor.*

*With a CBS cameraman recording the scene, cardinals and dignitaries line up to pay their respects to the newly installed Pope*

(S.) The just will shine out; as sparks run through the stubble, so will they.

(R.) *Antiphon.*

(S.) They shall judge nations, rule over peoples, and the Lord will be their King for ever.

(R.) *Antiphon.*

(S.) They who trust in him will understand the truth, those who are faithful will live with him in love.

(R.) *Antiphon.*

(S.) For grace and mercy await those he has chosen.

(R.) *Antiphon.*

*At the conclusion of the offertory, the Holy Father says the following prayer:*

Pray, brethren, that our sacrifice may be acceptable to God, the almighty Father.

(R.) *May the Lord accept the sacrifice at your hands, for the praise and glory of his name, for our good and for the good of all his Church.*

*Prayer over the gifts:*

Accept, O Father, our gifts for the Eucharistic sacrifice. Guard and protect your Holy Church, together with me your unworthy servant whom you have made its Pastor, through Christ our Lord.

(R.) *Amen.*

*If there are many concelebrants, they remain at their place. Only the first four concelebrants will come up to the altar, standing alongside the Pope. These will recite the delegated prayers.*

## PREFACE TO THE EUCHARISTIC PRAYER

(S.) The Lord be with you.

(R.) *And also with you.*

(S.) Lift up your hearts.

(R.) *We lift them up to the Lord.*

(S.) Let us give thanks to the Lord our God.

(R.) *It is right to give him thanks and praise.*

It is truly right and just, our duty and the source of salvation, to give thanks, always and everywhere, to you, Oh Lord, Holy Father, Almighty and eternal God:

At all times you give new energy to your Church and you guide it and protect it in a marvelous way throughout its history.

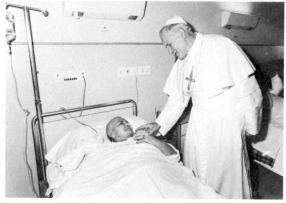

*In this poignant and moving picture, Pope John Paul II, the former Cardinal of Krakow, embraces Cardinal Wyszynski of Warsaw (upper photo). During a visit to a hospital in Rome, the Pope comforts Bishop Andrzej Maria Deskur*

By the power of your Holy Spirit you assure your Church of your support, with confident love the Church never fails to call on you in time of trouble. With joy, she always gives you thanks through Christ our Lord. In whom heaven and earth, the angels and archangels sing together with one voice:

*Acclamation:*

Holy, Holy, Holy Lord, God of power and might, heaven and earth are full of your glory. Hosanna in the highest. Blessed is he who comes in the name of the Lord. Hosanna in the highest.

*The Holy Father expresses the praise that all creatures and the people of the Church offer to God:*

Father, you are holy indeed, and all creation rightly gives you praise. All life, all holiness comes from you through your son, Jesus Christ our Lord, by the working of the Holy Spirit. From age to age you gather a people to yourself, so that from east to west a perfect offering may be made to the glory of your name.

The Holy Father and the Concelebrants invoke the Holy Spirit that the bread and wine become the Body and Blood of Christ:

And so, Father, we bring you these gifts. We ask you to make them holy by the power of your Spirit, that they may become the body and blood of your Son, our Lord Jesus Christ, at whose command we celebrate this eucharist.

*The Holy Father and the concelebrants re-present the sacrifice of Christ through the liturgical-sacramental signs.*

On the night he was betrayed, he took bread and gave you thanks and praise. He broke the bread, gave it to his disciples, and said: TAKE THIS, ALL OF YOU, AND EAT IT: THIS IS MY BODY WHICH WILL BE GIVEN UP FOR YOU.

*The Holy Father continues together with the concelebrants:*

When supper was ended, he took the cup. Again he gave you thanks and praise, gave the cup to his disciples, and said: TAKE THIS, ALL OF YOU, AND DRINK FROM IT: THIS IS THE CUP OF MY BLOOD, THE BLOOD OF THE NEW AND EVERLASTING COVENANT. IT WILL BE SHED FOR YOU AND FOR ALL MEN SO

*Some of the crowds thread their way past the impressive sculpture-like columns of Bernini's colonnade*

## THAT SINS MAY BE FORGIVEN. DO THIS IN MEMORY OF ME.

*The Holy Father says:*

**Let us proclaim the mystery of faith:**

*The assembly proclaims the Lord who died and rose again for our salvation.*

Christ has died, Christ is risen, Christ will come again.

*The Holy Father continues together with the concelebrants, by offering to the Father the sacrifice of the Son:*

**Father, calling to mind the death your Son endured for our salvation, his glorious resurrection and ascension into heaven, and ready to greet him when he comes again, we offer you in thanksgiving this holy and living sacrifice.**

*By invoking the Holy Spirit on all present:*

**Look with favor on your Church's offering, and see the Victim whose death has reconciled us to yourself. Grant that we, who are nourished by his body and blood, may be filled with his Holy Spirit, and become one body, one spirit in Christ.**

*One of the Concelebrants prays for the eternal salvation of those present:*

**May he make us an everlasting gift to you and enable us to share in the inheritance of your saints, with Mary, the Virgin Mother of God; with the apostles, the martyrs and all your saints, on whose constant intercession we rely for help.**

*Another one of the concelebrants asks for union for the Church and happiness for the deceased:*

**Lord, may this sacrifice, which has made our peace with you, advance the peace and salvation of all the world. Strengthen in faith and love your pilgrim Church on earth and all the bishops with the clergy and the entire people your Son has gained for you. Father, hear the prayers of the family you have gathered here before you. In mercy and love unite all your children wherever they may be.**

**Welcome into your kingdom our departed brothers and sisters, and all who have left this world in your friendship. We hope to enjoy forever the vision of your glory, through Christ our Lord, from whom all good things come.**

*A spectator reviews the candidates for election to the papacy; another uses the newspaper as a shield against the elements*

*Final Doxology — The Holy Father with the concelebrants:*

**Through him, with him, in him, in the unity of the Holy Spirit, all glory and honor is yours, almighty Father, for ever and ever.**

(R.)    *Amen.*

## THE COMMUNION RITE:

*Lord's Prayer*

*The Holy Father:* **Let us pray with confidence to the Father in the words our Saviour gave us:**

*The Holy Father and People:*

**Our Father, who art in heaven, hallowed be thy name; thy kingdom come; thy will be done on earth as it is in heaven; Give us this day our daily bread; and forgive us our trespasses as we forgive those who trespass against us; and lead us not into temptation, but deliver us from evil.**

*The Holy Father:*

**Deliver us, Lord, from every evil, and grant us peace in our day. In your mercy keep us free from sin and protect us from all anxiety as we wait in joyful hope for the coming of our Saviour, Jesus Christ.**

(R.)    *For the kingdom, the power, and the glory are yours, now and for ever.*

*The Kiss of Peace:*

*The Holy Father:* **Lord Jesus Christ, you said to your apostles: I leave you peace, my peace I give you. Look not on our sins, but on the faith of your Church, and grant us the peace and unity of your kingdom where you live for ever and ever.**

(R.)    *Amen.*

*The Holy Father:* **The peace of the Lord be with you always.**

(R.)    *And also with you.*

*Those present exchange a sign of peace, to be worthy to receive the Body and Blood of the Lord. While the Holy Father breaks the Eucharistic bread, the Schola and Assembly sing alternately:*

**Lamb of God, you take away the sins of the world: have mercy on us. Lamb of God, you take away the sins of the world: have mercy on us. Lamb of God, you take away the sins of the world: grant us peace.**

*The Holy Father elevates the Eucharistic Bread saying:*

*Magnificent statuary is everywhere present in the Vatican*

*Communicants wait their turn to receive the host from Pope John Paul II*

This is the Lamb of God who takes away the sins of the world. Happy are those who are called to his supper.

(R.)     *Lord, I am not worthy to receive you, but only say the word and I shall be healed.*

*The concelebrants receive the Body and Blood. And the faithful receive Holy Communion.*

*After the Holy Father has received communion, he will go in front of the altar accompanied by the Cardinal proto-deacon and the Master of Ceremonies to distribute communion. Meanwhile, a group of priests will be bringing communion to the congregation. During the distribution of communion, the choir will sing the communion canticle:*

Antiphon:     (John 12,36). **If a man serves me, he must follow me, wherever I am, my servant will be there too.**

(S.)     **I will bless Yahweh at all times, his praise shall be on my lips continually;**

(R.)     *Antiphon*

(S.)     **My soul glories in Yahweh, let the humble hear and rejoice.**

(R.)     *Antiphon.*

*When that is completed the Adoro te devote is sung: (Adoro te devote, ascribed to St. Thomas Aquinas (1227-1274); translated by Gerard Manley Hopkins (1844-1889).*

1.     *God-head here in hiding, whom I do adore; Masked by these bare shadows, shape and nothing more, See Lord, at thy service low lies here a heart; Lost, all lost in wonder at the God thou art.*

2.     *Seeing, touching, tasting are in thee deceived; How says trusty hearing? that shall be believed; What God's Son has told me, take for truth I do; Truth himself speaks truly or there's nothing true.*

3.     *On the cross thy god-head made no sign to men; Here thy very manhood steals from human ken: Both are my confession, both are my belief, And I pray the prayer made by the dying thief.*

4.     *I am not like Thomas, wounds I cannot see, But can plainly call thee Lord and God as he: This*

faith each day deeper be my holding of, Daily make me harder hope and dearer love.

5. O thou our reminder of Christ crucified, Living Bread the life of us for whom he died, Lend this life to me then: feed and feast my mind, There be thou the sweetness man was meant to find.

6. Bring the tender tale true of the Pelican; Bathe me, Jesus Lord, in what thy bosom ran — Blood that but one drop of has the world to win, All the world forgiveness of its world of sin.

7. Jesus whom I look at shrouded here below, I beseech thee send me what I thirst for so, Some day to gaze on thee, face to face in light, And be blest for ever with thy glory's sight.

After communion there is a brief period of silence. Then the Holy Father concludes the liturgy with the prayer after Communion and the blessing.

Oh, Lord, you have welcomed us at your table. Strengthen in love and unity your holy Church and me, your servant upon whom you have conferred the ministry of Supreme Pastor, so that together, flock and pastor, we may go forward securely along the path of salvation, through Christ our Lord.

(R.) Amen.

Acclamation: **Christ conquers, Christ reigns, Christ rules.**
(Repeated by Assembly)
**Christ, hear us.** (Repeated by Assembly).

(S.) **To our Pope, John Paull II, revered Pontiff of the Universal Church, may the Lord grant his blessings.**

(R.) May the Lord conserve him and protect him.

(S.) **For Pope John Paul II, Vicar of Christ, and for all the bishops of the Church, a long life.**

(R.) May the Lord grant him a long life, peace and fraternal charity in the unity of the Spirit.

(S.) **For Pope John Paul I, of revered memory, may the Lord grant eternal happiness and peace in the**

light of the Saints.

(R.) His memory is a blessing.

Christ conquers, Christ reigns, Christ rules.

Christ, hear us.

(S.) **For those in authority, to whom is entrusted the governing of nations and for all those who work for the common good, may theirs be untiring constancy in the search for peace and great success.**

(R.) May the blessing of the Lord be upon them all.

(S.) **For all the people who, in their faithfulness, adore the one true God, and for all men of good will, may the Lord grant peace, prosperity, and righteousness.**

(R.) For all the children of God may the Father grant light and love.

Christ conquers, Christ reigns, Christ rules.

To Christ alone be power, praise and glory for all ages.

(R.) Amen.

May our age be blessed.

(R.) May the peace of Christ be granted to all those redeemed by his blood.

Joyfully!

(R.) Joyfully, Joyfully.

May the kingdom of Christ come.

(R.) Thanks be to God. Amen.

The Cardinal Deacon then announces the plenary indulgence.

The Concluding Rite:

Holy Father: **The Lord be with you.**

(R.) And with your spirit.

Holy Father: **Blessed be the name of the Lord.**

(R.) Now and forever.

Holy Father: **Our help is in the name of the Lord.**

(R.) Who made heaven and earth.

Holy Father: **May Almighty God bless you, the Father, the son and the Holy Spirit.**

(R.) Amen.

Deacon: **Let us bless the Lord.**

(R.) Thanks be to God.

The papal choir intones the Te Deum. (Translation by Father Bernard Johnson O.C.S.O.)

(S.) **We praise you, O God, and we**

acknowledge you to be the Lord.

(R.) *All the earth adores you, Eternal Father.*

(S.) **All the angels and all the powers of heaven acknowledge you.**

(R.) *The Seraphim and Cherubim cry out to you with unceasing voices.*

(S.) **Holy,**

(R.) *Holy.*

(S.) **Holy, Lord God of Power.**

(R.) *Heaven and earth are full of the majesty of your glory.*

(S.) **The glorious chorus of Apostles praises you.**

(R.) *The worthy Prophets praise you.*

(S.) **The white-robed army of Martyrs praises you.**

(R.) *Holy Church throughout the world acknowledges you.*

(S.) **Father of immense majesty.**

(R.) *The true and venerable and Only-Begotten Son*

(S.) **And also the Holy Spirit, the Paraclete**

(R.) *You, O Christ, King of glory*

(S.) **You are the everlasting Son of the Father**

(R.) *When you undertook to free mankind, you did not disdain to be born of a Virgin.*

(S.) **Having conquered the sting of death, you opened the kingdom of heaven to all believers.**

(R.) *You sit at the right hand of God in the glory of the Father.*

(S.) **We believe that you will come as Judge.**

(R.) *Therefore we ask you to help your servants whom you have redeemed with your Precious Blood.*

(S.) **Let them be numbered among your saints in eternal glory.**

After the first verses, the Pope will kiss the altar and greet the prelates, the faithful in the Piazza and the Diplomatic Corps. Meanwhile the procession prepares to re-enter the Basilica with the Cardinals taking their place in the order of precedence. The procession will re-enter the Basilica and go towards the altar of the Pieta. The Cardinal concelebrants will gather to have a photo taken with the Holy Father. When that is completed the Pope will re-enter the sacristy of the Pieta and then will go to his apartment.

*Fully aware of the history-making occasion, Pope John Paul II and members of the press corps happily reach out to touch each other*

# Homily of John Paul II

**1** "You are the Christ, the Son of the living God" (Mt 16:16).

These words were spoken by Simon, son of Jonah, in the district of Caesarea Philippi. Yes, he spoke them with his own tongue, with a deeply lived and experienced conviction — but it is not in him that they find their source, their origin: ". . . because it was not flesh and blood that revealed this to you but my Father in heaven" (Mt 16:17). They were the words of Faith.

These words mark the beginning of Peter's mission in the history of salvation, in the history of the People of God. From that moment, from that confession of Faith, the sacred history of salvation and of the People of God was bound to take on a new dimension; to express itself in the historical dimension of the Church. This ecclesial dimension of the history of the People of God takes its origin, in fact is born, from these words of Faith, and is linked to the man who uttered them: "You are Peter — the rock — and on you, as on a rock, I will build my Church."

**2** On this day and in this place these same words must again be uttered and listened to:

"You are the Christ, the Son of the living God."

Yes, Brothers and Sons and Daughters, these words first of all.

Their content reveals to our eyes the mystery of the living God, the mystery to which the Son has brought us close. Nobody, in fact, has brought the living God close to men and revealed him as he alone did. In our knowledge of God, in our journey towards God, we are totally linked to the power of these words: "He who sees me sees the Father". He who is infinite, inscrutable, ineffable, has come close to us in Jesus Christ, the only-begotten Son of God, born of the Virgin Mary in the stable at Bethlehem.

All of you who are still seeking God,

All of you who already have the inestimable good fortune to believe,

And also you who are tormented by doubt:

Please listen once again, today in this sacred place, to the words uttered by Simon Peter. In those words is the faith of the Church. In those same words is the new truth, indeed, the ultimate and definitive truth about man: the son of the living God — "You are the Christ, the Son of the living God."

3 Today the new Bishop of Rome solemnly begins his ministry and the mission of Peter. In this City, in fact, Peter completed and fulfilled the mission entrusted to him by the Lord.

The Lord addressed him with these words:

"...when you were young you put on your own belt and walked where you liked; but when you grow old you will stretch out your hands and somebody else will put a belt round you and take you where you would rather not go" (Jn 21:18).

Peter came to Rome!

What else but obedience to the mandate received from the Lord guided him and brought him to this City, the heart of the Empire? Perhaps the fisherman of Galilee did not want to come here. Perhaps he would have preferred to stay there, on the shores of the Lake of Gennasaret, with his boat and his nets. But guided by the Lord, obedient to his mandate, he came here!

According to an ancient tradition (given magnificent literary expression in a novel by Henryk Sienkiewicz), during Nero's persecution Peter wanted to leave Rome. But the Lord intervened: he went to meet him. Peter spoke to him and asked: "Quo vadis, Domine?" — "Where are you going, Lord?" And the Lord answered him at once: "I am going to Rome to be crucified again". Peter went back to Rome and stayed here until his crucifixion.

Yes, Brothers and Sons and Daughters, Rome is the See of Peter. Down the centuries new Bishops continually succeeded him in this See. Today a new Bishop comes to the Chair of Peter in Rome, a Bishop full of trepidation, conscious of his unworthiness. And how could one not tremble before the greatness of this call and before the universal mission of this See of Rome!

To the See of Peter in Rome there succeeds today a Bishop who is not a Roman. *A Bishop who is a son of Poland.* But from this moment he too becomes a Roman. Yes — a Roman. He is a Roman also because he is the son of a nation whose history, from its first dawning, and whose thousand-year-old traditions are marked by a living, strong, unbroken and deeply felt link with the See of Peter, a nation which has ever remained faithful to this See of Rome. Inscrutable is the design of Divine Providence!

4 In past centuries, when the Successor of Peter took possession of his See, the *triregnum* or tiara was placed on his head. The last Pope to be crowned was Paul VI in 1963, but after the solemn coronation ceremony he never used the tiara again and left his Successors free to decide in this regard.

Pope John Paul I, whose memory is so vivid in our hearts, did not wish to have the tiara; nor does his Successor wish it today. This is not the time to return to a ceremony and an object considered wrongly to be a symbol of the temporal power of the Popes.

Our time calls us, urges us, obliges us to gaze on the Lord and immerse ourselves in humble and devout meditation on the mystery of the supreme power of Christ himself.

He who was born of the Virgin Mary, the carpenter's Son (as he was thought to be), the Son of the living God (confessed by Peter), came to make us all "a kingdom of priests".

The Second Vatican Council has reminded us of the mystery of this power and of the fact that Christ's mission as Priest, Prophet-Teacher and King continues in the Church. Everyone, the whole People of God, shares in this threefold mission. Perhaps in the past the tiara, this triple crown, was placed on the Pope's head in order to express by that symbol the Lord's plan for his Church, namely that all the hierarchical order of Christ's Church, all "sacred power" exercised in the Church is nothing other than service, service with a single purpose: to ensure that all the People of God share in this threefold mission of Christ and always remain under the power of the Lord, a power that has its source not in the powers of this world but in the mystery of the Cross and Resurrection.

The absolute and yet sweet and gentle power of the Lord responds to the whole depths of the human person, to his loftiest aspirations of intellect, will and heart. It does not speak the language of force but expresses itself in charity and truth.

The new Successor of Peter in the See of Rome today makes a fervent, humble and trusting prayer: Christ, make me become and remain the servant of your unique power, the servant of your power that knows no eventide. Make me be a servant. Indeed, the servant of your servants.

5 Brothers and Sisters, do not be afraid to welcome Christ and accept his power. Help the Pope and all those who wish to serve Christ and with Christ's power to serve the human person and the whole of mankind. Do not be afraid. Open wide the doors for Christ. To his saving power open the boundaries of States, economic and political systems, the vast fields of culture, civilization and development. Do not be afraid. Christ knows "what is in man." He alone knows it.

So often today man does not know what is within him, in the depths of his mind and heart. So often he is uncertain about the meaning of his life on this earth. He is assailed by doubt, a doubt which turns into despair. We ask you therefore, we beg you with humility and trust, let Christ speak to man. He alone has words of life, yes, of eternal life.

Precisely today the whole Church is celebrating "World Mission Day"; that is, she is praying, meditating and acting in order that Christ's words of life may reach all people and be received by them as a message of hope, salvation and total liberation.

6 I thank all of you here present who have wished to participate in this solemn inauguration of the ministry of the new Successor of Peter.

I heartily thank the Heads of State, the Representatives of the Authorities, and the Government Delegations for so honouring me with their presence.

Thank you, Eminent Cardinals of the Holy Roman Church.

I thank you, my beloved Brothers in the Episcopate.

Thank you, Priests.

To you, Sisters and Brothers, Religious of the Orders and Congregations, I give my thanks.

Thank you, people of Rome.

Thanks to the pilgrims who have come here from all over the world.

Thanks to all of you who are linked with this Sacred Ceremony by radio and television.

7 I speak to you, my dear Fellow-countrymen, Pilgrims from Poland, Brother Bishops with your magnificent Primate at your head, Priests, Sisters and Brothers of the Polish Religious Congregations — to you representatives of Poland from all over the world.

What shall I say to you who have come from my Krakow, from the See of Saint Stanislaus of whom I was the unworthy successor for fourteen years? What shall I say? Everything that I could say would fade into insignificance compared with what my heart feels, and your hearts feel, at this moment.

So let us leave aside words. Let there remain just great silence before God, the silence that becomes prayer. I ask you: be with me! At Jasna Gora and everywhere. Do not cease to be with the Pope who today prays with the words of the poet: "Mother of God, you who defend Bright Czestochowa and shine at Ostrobrama." And these same words I address to you at this particular moment.

8 That was an appeal and a call to prayer for the new Pope, an appeal expressed in the Polish language. I make the same appeal to all the sons and daughters of the Catholic Church. Remember me today and always in your prayers!

I open my heart to all my Brothers of the Christian Churches and Communities, and I greet in particular you who are here present, in anticipation of our coming personal meeting; but for the moment I express to you my sincere appreciation for your having wished to attend this solemn ceremony.

And I also appeal to all men — to every man (and with what veneration the apostle of Christ must utter this word; "man!")

— pray for me!

— help me to be able to serve you! Amen.

# 5
# SPEECHES OF JOHN PAUL II

As a stunned and amazed world anxiously crowded either into St. Peter's Square or in front of television sets, the newly elected Polish Pope prepared to further acquaint himself with the faithful, the curious, and the proud.

A wise and beneficent man, the former Cardinal Wojtyla, impressed everyone with his loving Message to the World in which he stressed both the importance of continuing to implement the terms of Vatican II and the necessity of collegiality — all bishops sharing the responsibility of the Living Church.

In his address to the Cardinals, after the Pontiff expressed gratitude for his election as the "Successor to Peter in the See of Rome," he asked that the bishops be "linked, one to the other and should show concern for all of the churches." Obviously, he expects, and will receive their help in implementing his policies.

Because of his high church position in Poland, constantly fighting and placating the Communist government to gain concessions for the Catholic population, John Paul II's Address to the Diplomatic Corps was poignant, yet meaningful when he asked for a world full of justice and peace.

Not only did the new Pope deliver a blessing and address to the Press; he held an impromptu press conference, answering the questions of each journalist in the appropriate language. By so doing, he gained the lasting affection of the international journalists, photographers, cameramen, and broadcasters whose jobs are always difficult at best.

# Message to the Church and to the World

Reverend Cardinals, Sons and Daughters of the Holy Church, All Men of Good Will, who now listen

Only one word, among so many others, comes immediately to our lips in this moment. We present ourselves to you after our election to the See of the Apostle Peter, and the word that comes to mind — in evident contrast with our personal and human limitations before the immense responsibility entrusted to us is: "How rich are the depths of God—how deep his wisdom and knowledge—and how impossible to penetrate his motives or understand his methods!" (Rom 11.33) In fact, who could have foreseen, after the death of our unforgettable Paul VI, the premature departure of his lovable successor, John Paul I? How would we have been able to foresee that this formidable heritage would have passed to our shoulders? Therefore we must meditate on the mysterious design of the provident God, the good God — not to understand — but rather to adore and to pray. We feel the need to repeat the invocation of the Psalmist, who, raising his eyes upward, exclaimed "When I am in trouble, I call to Yahweh, and He answers me." (Psalm 120,1-2

These events, which no one foresaw, happening in so brief a time, and the inadequacy with which we can respond to that expectation urges us not only to turn to the Lord and to trust completely in him, but also prevents us from outlining programs for our Pontificate which would be the fruit of long reflection and careful development. But to make up for this, there is already something present. It is the sign of the comforting presence of God.

It is less than a month since all of us, both inside and outside these historic walls of the Sistine Chapel, heard the allocution of Pope John Paul, at the very beginning of his promising ministry as Supreme Pastor. The memory is so fresh that each one of us holds it close. Considering the wisdom of the points contained therein, it is not possible to prescind from it. Remembering the circumstances in which it was presented, it is right to recall it here at the beginning of a new pontificate. With it, we bind ourselves in the presence of God and the Church.

We want, therefore, to highlight some direct points that we hold in prominence. On our part — as we propose and hope with the help of the Lord — these matters not only hold our attention and consent — but they also are specially compelling, corresponding as they do with the ecclesial reality.

Above all, we want to insist on the constant importance of the Second Vatican Council. For us, it is a formal obligation that it be studiously put into effect. Is not the Council a milestone in the two-thousand-year history of the Church, and, indeed, in the religious and cultural history of the world? But just as the Council is not contained merely in documents, neither is it put into effect by the implementation which has taken place in these so-called post-Council years. We consider, therefore, our primary duty that of promoting, with prudent, but encouraging action, the most exact execution of the norms and the directives of the Council. Above all we favor the development of a proper mentality. First it is necessary to place one's self in harmony with the Council. One must put into practice what was stated; and what was "implicit" should be made explicit in light of the experimentation that followed and in conjunction with emerging, new circumstances.

It is essential, in a word, that the fertile seeds which the Fathers of the Second Vatican Council, nourished by the Word of God, sowed in the good earth (Mt 13, 8-23) should grow to maturity, a maturity of movement and of life. By the seed is meant their authoritative teachings and their pastoral deliberations.

This general thrust of faithfulness to the Second Vatican Council and the express intention on our part to put it into effect embraces many aspects. There are the missionary and the ecumenical aspects; there are disciplinary and organizational aspects, but one aspect above all others — the one that calls for the closest attention, is that of ecclesiology (the theology of the Church). Venerable Brothers and beloved Sons and Daughters of the Catholic world, it is necessary to take hold again of that "Magna Carta" of the Council, the dogmatic Constitution, "Lumen Gentium". We must make a renewed and strengthened meditation on the nature and the function of the Church, on its mode of being and of acting — and this not merely to develop still more perfectly that living communion in Christ of all who hope and believe in Him, but also to contribute to a fuller and closer unity within the whole human race. Pope John XXIII used to love to repeat the words: "The Church of Christ is the light of the nations". The Church — and here the Council echoed this truth — is the universal sacrament of salvation and of unity for the human race (cf Lumen Gentium n. 1.48; Dec. Ad Gentes, no.1).

The mystery of salvation which finds its center in the Church and is actualized through the Church, the dynamism, which on account of that same mystery, animates the People of God, the special bond or collegiality which "with Peter and under Peter" binds together the Bishops; all these are elements on which we have not yet sufficiently reflected. We must do so in order to decide in face of human needs, whether permanent or passing, what the Church should adopt as its mode of presence and its course of action. To have both a clearly marked path and a driving stimulus all of us, Bishops and faithful, must always adhere to the teachings of the Council, seen in the light of tradition and placed in harmony with the dogmatic formulations arrived at a century ago by the First Vatican Council. This way too, we repeat, we are able to walk towards life and on the road of history.

In a special way we urge a deeper reflection on the implications of collegiality, so that our minds might be better informed and that we might undertake our responsibilities more conscientiously. The bond of collegiality closely links the Bishops to the successor of Peter and to each other. Thus, they carry out their function of bringing the light of the Gospel to the world, of sanctifying it by the instruments of grace and of guiding with pastoral care the whole people of God.

Collegiality undoubtedly means that there will be appropriate development of those bodies, sometimes new, sometimes up-dated, which can secure a better union of heart, of will, of activity in building up the Body of Christ which is the Church (cf Eph. 4, 12: Col. 1,24). In this regard, we make special mention of the Synod of Bishops, first established before the Council came to an end by that man of immense genius, Paul VI (cf Litt. Ap. Apostolica Sollicitudo, motu proprio datas: AAS LVII/1965, pp 775-780).

Over and above our reference to the Council, there remains the responsibility for total fidelity to the mission which we have received and which above all binds us. At this point in the discourse, what applies to others is valid also for us, and therefore we speak in the first person.

Called as we are to the supreme responsibility in the Church, it is above all we who are obliged to be an example of willingness and of action. We must express with all our strength this fidelity. We must always keep intact the deposit of faith, mindful of the special mandate of Christ who, making Simon the "Rock" on which he built the Church, gave him the keys of the kingdom of heaven (cfr Mt. 16, 18-19). He commanded him to strengthen his brothers (cfr Lk. 22, 32) and to feed the sheep and lambs of his flock (cfr John 21, 15-17) as a witness of love. We are completely convinced that all modern enquiry into the "Petrine Ministry" must be based on these three hinges of the Gospel. What is proper and peculiar to it becomes clearer day by day. We are dealing here with individual facets of the office which are connected with the very nature of the Church to preserve its internal unity and to guarantee her spiritual mission. This has been entrusted not only to Peter but also to his legitimate successor. We are convinced also that this most singular mission must be done always in love. Love is the source which nourishes and the climate in which one grows. It is the necessary response to the question of Jesus, "Do you love me?"

We repeat therefore, with St. Paul: "The love of Christ urges us on". (2 Cor. 5, 14) because we wish our ministry to be a ministry of love; we wish it to be so in its every expression and manifestation. Our purpose now is to follow in the school of our immediate predecessors. Who does not remember the words of Pope Paul VI, who preached a "civilization of love"; and about a month before his death, he re-affirmed with all his heart "I have kept the faith." (cfr Homily for the feast of Sts. Peter and Paul in AAS LXX 1978 pg 395 .) He did not do so for self praise but, rather that after fifteen years of service in his apostolic ministry, he might thoroughly and religiously examine his conscience. And what can we say of John Paul I? It seems that almost yesterday he left our ranks to take on the weight of the Papacy, but what warmth! It was a true "wave of love" that he gave the world in his last greeting at the Sunday Angelus — this he offered to the world in the few days of his ministry. He confirmed it by his wise teaching on faith, on hope and on love during his public audiences.

Venerable brothers, dear sons and daughters, it is obvious that fidelity also demands adherence to the teaching of Peter especially in the field of doctrine. The objective importance of the "magisterium" should always be kept in mind and safe guarded. In our age, there appears here and there dangers to certain truths of the Catholic faith. Fidelity also means respect for liturgical norms issued by Church authorities. It excludes therefore either arbitrary and uncontrolled innovation or the resistance to that which have been legitimately prescribed and introduced in the Sacred Rites.

Faithfulness indicates also respect for the great discipline of the Church. This too, as you remember, was spoken of by our Predecessor. Discipline isn't aimed only at mortification, but also as a guarantee for the correct ordering proper to the Mystical Body. It assures the customary and natural relationship among all the members who make up that body. Fidelity signifies furthermore a generous cooperation with the demands of the priestly and religious vocation in a way that what is freely promised to God will always be maintained and developed, in asmuch as life is viewed always from a supernatural perspective.

For the faithful, finally, as the word itself indicates, faithfulness should be a natural responsibility of their being Christians. They should profess their faith with a prompt and loyal spirit. They should witness it both by obedience to their sacred Pastors whom the Holy Spirit has placed to shepherd the Church (cf Acts 20, 28) and by collaborating in those initiatives and tasks to which they have been called.

At this point, we cannot forget our Brothers of other Churches and Christian Confessions. The ecumenical cause is actually so great and delicate that we cannot now let it go unmentioned. How many times have we meditated together on the last will of Christ, that asks the Father for his disciples the gift of unity (John 17, 21-23)? And who does not recall the insistence of St. Paul on the "communion of the spirit" which leads one to be united in love with a common purpose and a common mind in the imitation of Christ the Lord (cf Philippians 2, 2.5-8)? It does not seem possible that there would still remain the drama of the division among Christians — a cause of confusion and perhaps even of scandal. We intend, therefore, to proceed along the way already begun, by favoring those steps which serve to remove obstacles.

Hopefully, then, thanks to a common effort, we might arrive finally at full communion.

We desire, furthermore, to turn to all men who, as sons of the Omnipotent God, are our brothers in love and service. We say to them without presumption, but with sincere humility, that we desire to make an effective contribution to the cause of permanent and prevailing peace, of development, of international justice. We have no intention of political interference, nor of participation in the working out of temporal affairs. Just as the Church excludes being contained within the categories of earthly order, so our responsibility in approaching these burning questions of men and of nations shall be determined only by religious and moral motivation. Follow Him who said to his followers that the ideal of their life is to be "salt of the earth" and "light of the world" (Mt 5, 13-16). We intend to work for the consolidation of spiritual supports on which human society can build. This duty seems more urgent for us now in light of the ongoing inequalities and misunderstandings, which, in turn, are the cause of tensions and conflicts in many parts of the world. They bear within themselves the further threat of added inhuman catastrophes. Constant, therefore, shall be our concern, faced with such problems. Inspired by the Gospel, we will seek timely, unprejudiced action.

It is good to take to heart at this moment the grave problem which the College of Cardinals addressed during the Sede Vacante — that regarding the beloved land of Lebanon and its people who earnestly desire peace and liberty. At the same time we would like to reach out our hands and open our hearts in this moment, to all people and to those who are oppressed by whatever injustices or discrimination whether it has to do with economy, life in society, political life or the freedom of conscience and just religious freedom. We must reach out with all means to them, that all forms of injustice manifest in our times be rejected by public opinion. May they be remedied, so that all might live a life worthy of man. That which is part of the mission of the Church as seen in the Second Vatican Council, and not only in the dogmatic Constitution *Lumen Gentium* but, also in the pastoral Constitution *Gaudium et Spes*, has been brought to light.

Brothers, dear sons and daughters, the recent happenings of the Church and of the world are for us all a healthy warning: How will our pontificate be? What is the destiny the Lord has assigned to His Church in the years to come? What road will humanity take as it approaches the year 2000? These are burning questions. The only answer is: "God knows" (cf Cor. 12, 2-3).

Our personal fate which has brought us unexpectedly to the heaviest responsibility of apostolic service is of little significance. Our person — we ought to say — must be lost as we confront the weighty office we must fill. And so a speech must be changed into an appeal. After praying to the Lord, we feel it necessary to beg your prayers to gain that indispensable, higher strength that will make it possible for us to take up the work of our predecessors from the point where they left off. After acknowledging their cherished memory, we offer to each one of you, the Cardinals, who chose us for this responsibility, a greeting which is sincere and grateful. We extend a greeting which is both trusting and encouraging to all our brothers in the Episcopacy, to the bishops who in different parts of the world preside over the care of the individual churches, the chosen sections of the People of God (cf Dec. Christus Dominus no. 11) and who are co-workers with us in the work of universal salvation. Behind them, we acknowledge the order of priesthood, the band of missionaries, the companies of religious men and women. At the same time we earnestly hope that their numbers will grow, echoing in our mind those words of the Saviour, "The harvest is great, the laborers are few" (Mt 9,37-38); (Lk: 10,2). Then we turn again to the families and to Christian communities, to the many associations of the Apostolate, to the faithful who, even if they are not known individually to us, are not anonymous, not strangers, not marginal — never — they will be in the glorious company of the Church of Christ.

# Talk to the Cardinals

Venerable Brothers,

What can I say — what do I wish to say to you in this meeting when we are still certainly moved by the ecclesial events of these days?

Above all, I thank the Cardinal Dean for the noble words he has spoken representing your sentiments; and I am especially grateful for the expression of unique trust that you have placed in my humble person by electing me as Successor to Peter in the See of Rome. Only in the light of faith is it possible to accept with inner peace and with trust the fact that, in virtue of your choice, I have become the Vicar of Christ on earth and the visible head of the Church.

Venerable brothers, it was an act of trust and, at the same time, an act of courage to have wished to call a "non-Italian" to be Bishop of Rome. One can do nothing else but bow one's head to such a decision by the Sacred College.

Perhaps never so much as in these recent events in the life of the Church, whereby, within two months we have twice been deprived of our universal pastor, has the Christian people felt and experienced the importance, delicacy, responsibility of the tasks which have to be undertaken by the Sacred College of Cardinals; and never so much as in this period of time — we should recognize it with true satisfaction — have the faithful demonstrated such an affectionate esteem and so much benevolent understanding for your Eminences. The fervent and prolonged applause given to you at the end of the Mass "For the Election of the Pope" and at the announcement of the election of the new Pope were a most expressive, uplifting and moving proof of this.

The faithful have truly understood, Venerable brothers, that the scarlet you wear is a sign of that faithfulness which you promised the Pope in the solemn oath "even to the shedding of blood." Yours is a vestment of blood, which recalls and represents the blood that the Apostles, the Bishops, the Cardinals have shed for Christ during the course of the centuries. At this moment the figure of a great Bishop, St. John Fisher, comes to mind. He was created Cardinal — as is known — while he ws imprisoned for his faithfulness to the Pope of Rome. On the morning of June 22, 1535, while preparing to offer his head to the axe of the executioner, turning to the crowd, he exclaimed, "Christian people, I am going immediately to my death for my faith in the Holy Catholic Church of Christ." I would also have to add that even in our time there are those who have not been spared and still are not spared from the experience of prison, of suffering of humiliation for Christ.

May this inconquerable faithfulness to the spouse of Jesus be the distinctive honor and the pre-eminent boast of the College of Cardinals.

There is another element that I would wish to underline in this brief meeting: *a sense of brotherhood*, which in these recent days was evermore manifest and binding among the Sacred College. "Oh how good and how joyful for brothers to dwell together as one." (Psalm 1, 32, 1.) The Sacred College had to face, on two occasions and in a very brief span of time, one of the most delicate problems for the Church: that of electing the Roman Pontiff. And on that occasion the authentic universality of the Church showed forth. One can truly realize the extent St. Augustine affirms: "The Church, herself, speaks the language of all nations .... the Church spread throughout the nations speaks with all tongues." (*Tract on the Gospel of John XXXII,7: PL 35, 1645*.)

The experiences, the needs, the complex ecclesial problems are various and indeed frequently diverse. But such variety has been — and certainly will be — always *bound together in one unique faith*, as that same Bishop of Hippo recalled when he stressed the beauty and variety of the vestiture of the Queen-Church: "These languages create a variety of vestiture for this Queen. But just as every variety of vestiture should blend in unity, thus all languages lead to one faith." (*Narration on Psalm XLIV*, 23: *PL* 36, 509.)

It would be difficult for me not to express also deep gratitude to our Holy Father, Pope Paul VI, for the fact that he wished to give to the Sacred College a dimension that was broad, international and inter-continental. Its members indeed come from the extreme ends of the earth. This allows proof not only for the universality of the Church but also the universal quality of the City (of Rome).

In a few days you will be returning to your positions of responsibility; the majority of you to your diocese; others to the dicastery of the Holy See; all to continue your pastoral ministry with an ever increasing commitment, marked by responsibility, by worries, by sacrifice, but also comforted by the grace of the Lord and the spiritual joy that He gives to those who serve his faithful.

But even as the head of particular churches, you always share in solicitude for the entire Church, by living and by realizing with all your strength how much the Second Vatican Council asks of you: "As lawful successors of the Apostles and as members of the Episcopal College, Bishops should always realize that they are linked, one to the other and should show concern for all of the churches. For by divine institution and the requirements of their Apostolic office, each one, in concert with his fellow Bishops, is responsible for the Church." (*Christus Dominus* No. 6; cfr. *Ibid*, No. 3; *Lumen Gentium*, 23.)

Invoking on all of you, on the faithful bound to your pastoral zeal and on those dear to you, the grace of Christ and the vigilant protection of Mary, the "Mother of the Church," I would wish to impart with great affection my Apostolic Benediction. I would wish to do it first for you and then with all of you and thus the Church will be blessed everywhere by the new Bishop of Rome and by the entire College of Cardinals whose members come from every part of the world and yet are so close to Him.

# Address to the Diplomatic Corps

We are very touched by the noble words, the kind sentiments which your spokesman has addressed to us. We know the relationship, filled with esteem and mutual confidence, which had been established between Pope Paul VI and each of the diplomatic representations accredited to the Holy See. The climate created was one filled with understanding, respectful and benevolent; for that great Pope had the responsibility of pursuing the common good of peoples, and above all of pursuing it in keeping with the higher ideals which animate peace and development. Our immediate predecessor, dear Pope John Paul I, in receiving you less than two months ago, began a similar relationship. Each of you still remembers his words filled with humility, with his own readiness, with a pastoral sensitivity. We would make these entirely our own. And so today we inherit that same responsibility and you, you express to us the same confidence with the same enthusiasm. We thank you heartily for those sentiments which in extending them to our person, you are witnessing faithfulness to the Holy See as well.

May each of you feel yourself to be cordially welcome here at this instant. It is a welcome that is extended to you personally, to your country, and to the people whom you represent. Yes, if there is a place where all peoples should come together in peace and mutual respect, with sensitivity, with a sincere desire for their dignity, their goodness, their progress, it is certainly at the heart of the Church, near the Holy See, established to give witness to the truth and love of Christ. Our esteem and our good wishes then go to each and to all of you in your diverse circumstances. In this meeting there are actually represented not only governments but also peoples and nations. Among them there are the old nations endowed with a great past, with a fertile history, with their own traditions and cultures. There are also the young nations which have just recently sprung up, some with great possibilities of achievement; others just now awakening and being formed. The Church always desires to share in the life of as well as to contribute to the development of peoples and of nations. The Church has always recognized the special richness in the diversity and plurality of their cultures, their histories, their languages. In many cases the Church has specifically played its own part in the formation of these cultures. The Church has believed and continued to believe that in international situations, it is necessary to respect the rights of each nation.

For us, called from one of these nations to succeed the Apostle Peter in the service of the Universal Church and all the nations, we intend to manifest to each the esteem that it is their right to expect. You should then share our fervent wishes with those who govern you and with your fellow citizens. Here it is true to say that the individuality of our country of origin no longer is of great importance: as a Christian, even more as Pope, we are, we will be, the witness of universal love. We have for all the same good will but especially for those who undergo trial. When one speaks of diplomatic relations, one speaks of stable relationships, mutual, conducted with courtesy, with discretion, with loyalty. Without confusing competencies, they manifest on our part not necessarily the approval of one or another regime — that is not our affair — nor evidently the approval of all their actions in the conduct of public affairs; but rather an appreciation of the positive temporal values, a willingness to dialogue with those who are legitimately charged with the common good of society, an understanding of their role which is often difficult, an interest and an assistance for those human causes which are theirs to promote; sometimes this is achieved by direct intervention, but above all by the formation of consciences, a contribution specific to justice and peace at the international level.

In doing this the Holy See does not wish to depart from its pastoral role: intent on putting into practice the concern of Christ, in preparing the eternal salvation for human beings, which is its first duty, how could it be disinterested in the well-being and in the progress of peoples in this world?

On the other hand, the Church and the Holy See in particular wants your nations, your governments to always take into consideration a certain number of needs. The Holy See seeks nothing for itself, it works, in union with the local episcopacy, for the Christians or believers who dwell in your countries, so that without special privilege, but in all justice, they might nourish their faith, be guaranteed religious worship, and be admitted, as loyal citizens to participate fully in social life. The Holy See does so equally in the interest of men whomever they be, knowing that liberty, respect for life and the dignity of persons — who are never instruments — equality in treatment, professional conscientiousness in the task and united pursuit of the common good, the spirit of reconciliation, an opening towards spiritual values; these are the fundamental needs for harmonious life in society, for progress of citizens and for their civilization. Certainly these immediate objectives provide the outline for a program for responsible people. But the end result is not yet achieved; and all the means are not equally valuable. There are still too many physical and moral miseries resulting from negligence, from egoism, blindness or the hardness of men. The Church wants to help remove these sufferings through peaceful means, in educating towards moral sensitivity, by the loyal activity of Christians and of all men of good will. In doing this, the Church might sometimes not be understood but it is committed to providing a service which humanity cannot do without: it is faithful to its Master and Saviour, Jesus Christ. It is in this spirit that we hope to maintain and develop with all the countries whom you represent, relationships that are cordial and fruitful. We encourage you in your lofty responsibility; we encourage above all that your Governments always seek greater justice and peace, in a love that is well understood by your fellow citizens and in an openness of spirit and of heart towards other peoples. On that path may God enlighten you and strengthen you, both you personally and all those who are in a position of authority; and may he bless each of your countries.

# Commentary to the Press

Ladies and Gentlemen,

I bid you welcome! And thank you heartily for everything you have done, and for everything you will do, to present to the general public, in the press, on the radio, and on television, the events in the Catholic Church which have gathered you several times at Rome within the last two months.

Certainly, at the mere professional level, you have lived through days as tiring as they were moving. The sudden, unforeseeable character of the facts that followed one another obliged you to appeal to a sum of knowledge in the area of religious information that was, perhaps, unfamiliar to you; and then to meet, under conditions that were sometimes feverish, a requirement marked by the malady of the century: haste. For you, to wait for the white smoke was not a restful hour!

Thank you in the first place for having echoed so widely, with unanimous respect, the extensive and really historic labour of the great Pope Paul VI. Thank you for having made so familiar the smiling face and the evangelical attitude of my immediate predecessor, John Paul I. Thank you again for the favorable coverage you gave to the recent conclave, to my election and to the first steps I have taken in the heavy office of the pontificate. In any case, it was an opportunity for you not only to speak of persons — who pass — but of the See of Rome, of the Church, her traditions and her rites, her faith, her problems and her hopes, of St. Peter and the role of the Pope, of the great spiritual stakes of today: in short, of the mystery of the Church. Allow me to dwell a little on this aspect: it is difficult to present well the true face of the Church.

Yes, it is always difficult to read events, and to enable others to read them. In the first place they are nearly always complex. It is enough for an element to be forgotten inadvertently, omitted deliberately, minimized or on the contrary emphasized disproportionately, to distort the present vision and the forecasts to come. Ecclesial events, furthermore, are more difficult to grasp for those who contemplate them — I say it in all respect for everyone — outside a vision of faith, and even more difficult to express to a large public which has difficulty in perceiving their real meaning. You must, nevertheless, arouse the interest and win a hearing from this public, while your agencies ask you often and above all for the sensational. Some are then tempted to drop into the anecdote: it is concrete and it may be very good, but on condition that the anecdote is significant and really related to the nature of the religious phenomenon. Others plunge courageously into a very advanced analysis of the problems and motives of ecclesial persons, with the risk of not considering sufficiently the essential which, as you know, is not of a political but of a spiritual nature. Finally, from this last point of view, things are often more simple than is imagined: I hardly dare speak of my election!

But this is not the time to examine in detail all the risks and merits of your task as reporters of religious news. Let us note, moreover, that here and there some progress seems to be visible in pursuit of the truth, and in understanding and presentation of the religious phenomenon. I congratulate you on the part you have played in it.

But this is not the time to examine in detail all the risks and merits of your task as reporters of religious news. Let us note, moreover, that here and there some progress seems to be visible in pursuit of the truth, and in understanding and presentation of the religious phenomenon. I congratulate you on the part you have played in it.

Perhaps you yourselves have been surprised and encouraged by the importance attributed to it, in all countries, by a very wide public which some people thought was indifferent or allergic to the ecclesiastical institution and to spiritual things. In actual fact, the handing down of the supreme office, entrusted by Christ to St. Peter, with regard to all the peoples to be evangelized and to all the disciples of Christ to be gathered in unity, really appeared as a reality transcending habitual events. Yes, the handing down of this office has a deep echo in spirits and in hearts which perceive that God is at work in history. It was loyal to acknowledge it and to adapt to it the media of social communication which, in different degrees, you have at your disposal.

It is my wish precisely that craftsmen of religious information may always find the help they need from competent ecclesial organisms. The latter must receive them in respect for their convictions and their profession, supply them with very adequate and very objective documentation, but also propose to them a Christian perspective which sets facts in their true significance for the Church and for mankind. In this way you will be able to tackle these religious reports with the specific competence that they demand.

You are very concerned about freedom of information and of expression: you are right. Think yourselves lucky to enjoy it! Use this freedom well to grasp the truth more closely and to admit your readers, your listeners or viewers into "whatever is true, whatever is honorable, whatever is just, whatever is pure, whatever is lovely, whatever is gracious," to repeat the words of St. Paul (Ph. 4:8); into what helps them to live in justice and brotherhood, to discover the ultimate meaning of life, to open them up to the mystery of God, so near each of us. Under these conditions, your profession, so demanding and sometimes so exhausting — I was going to say your vocation — so topical and so beautiful will elevate further the spirit and the heart of men of good will, at the same time as the faith of Christians. It is a service which the Church and humanity appreciate.

I venture to call upon you also to an effort of comprehension, as to a loyal pact: when you report on the life and activity of the Church, try even more to grasp the authentic, deep and spiritual motivations of the Church's thought and action. The Church, on her side, listens to the objective testimony of journalists on the expectations and demands of this world. That does not mean, of course, that she models her message on the world of her time: it is the Gospel that must always inspire her attitude.

I am happy at this first contact with you. I assure you of my understanding and I take the liberty of relying on yours. I know that in addition to your professional problems, to which we will come back another time, you each have your personal and family cares. Let us not be afraid to entrust them to the Virgin Mary, who is always at Christ's side. And in Christ's name, I willingly bless you.

The Holy Father then continued in English:

I would like to offer my greetings and my blessing, not only to you, but to all your colleagues throughout the world. Although you represent different cultures, you are all united in the service of truth. And the corps that you make up here today is, in itself, a splendid manifestation of unity and solidarity. I would ask to be remembered to your families and to your fellow citizens in your respective countries. Please accept — all of you — my expression of respect, esteem and fraternal love.

# 6 | A FUTURE VISION

In the last twenty years, the Roman Catholic Church has undergone great changes, the likes of which had not been experienced since the Protestant Reformation over 400 years ago.

Not the least of these turnabouts is the election of a successor to St. Peter as Bishop of Rome of a man, as he said himself, from afar — a Polish Cardinal, Karol Wojtyla, the first non-Italian Holy Father in over 455 years. Yet as the fine figure of the smiling and joyful Holy Father appeared on the balcony of St. Peter's to let the world see the new Successor of the Prince of the Apostles for the first time, all suddenly realized that he was now taking possession of the same Roman Catholic Church as every one of his 263 predecessors had done since the appointment of St. Peter.

In all those centuries not one of the Church's fundamental beliefs had been changed; not one of its basic rules had been modified in its bi-millennial history.

What had undergone great adaptation was the outward show of the institution, and even here the changes were superficial. The Church was still a monarchical society with the Pope or Holy Father as its supreme pastor. Each diocese was still under the total guidance of its bishop as a successor to the apostles.

From the window in the upper room where the Holy Spirit appeared above the heads of the disciples and the Blessed Mother, Peter had told these new Christians to take the good news of the gospel back with them to the communities of Palestine, Syria, Asia Minor, Greece, and Rome from whence they had come to Jerusalem for the high holy days. Thus the whole world of that day had heard of Jesus Christ — dead and risen from the dead — from these devout Christians from all over their world. They gave the primitive church its catholic or universal presence that it has preserved down through the centuries.

*In his first talk with members of the international press corps, the Holy Father promised the cooperation of the Vatican to assure accurate and comprehensive reporting of religious news*

Today as Pope John Paul II looks out from the windows of the Vatican and contemplates the 725 millions of Catholics and the other hundreds of millions of Christians who are scattered all over the world, he knows that one of his first and most important tasks is to pursue the unity of faith and love among Christians that Christ prayed for so earnestly.

Then as he said explicitly in the talk he gave to the whole world after his first mass as Pope, he would devote himself fully to removing the scandal of Christian disunity and then spread the message of the love of neighbor to all mankind. This would include the love that Christians should have for non-Christians, Jews, non-believers, believers of the Oriental religions, and all men of goodwill.

In this program John Paul II was, of course, carrying out the designs of his two great predecessors: Pope John XXIII who inaugurated Vatican Council II for the very purpose of beginning a truly world-wide thrust toward Christian unity, and of Pope Paul VI who brought the Council to a successful close in 1965.

Finally, in projecting a great joyous spirit as Pope and Holy Father, going out of his way to greet as many of the ordinary people who came to Rome to see him at his inauguration and in the various audiences he gave during his first weeks as Pope, John Paul II was fully imitating the tactics of his immediate short-lived predecessor John Paul I who wanted to show everyone how much, as a Christian, he loved his neighbor as himself.

As John Paul II began his papal ministry, Cardinal Pericle Felici placed on his shoulders the woolen pallium — a symbol of pastoral responsibility. The white lamb stole with black Latin crosses reminds the world that Christ proclaimed himself the good shepherd and was pictured by the primitive church as carrying a lamb on his shoulders. Even more so, it is the constant recalling to the Holy Father of Christ's command to Peter: "Feed my lambs and feed my sheep."

In taking control of the church's institutional structure, Pope John Paul II had no intention of letting papal authority fall by the wayside. He meant, however, to exercise that authority not as a political figure but rather as a pastor of souls governing with Christ's authority who said "all authority in heaven and on earth is given to me." Then turning to his apostles, Christ had said, "whatever you lose on earth shall be loosed in heaven and whatever you bind on earth shall be bound in heaven."

Combining that spiritual authority with the specific command given to his predecessor Peter "and you once strengthen (in faith) confirm your brethren," Pope John Paul II intends, again as he told the Cardinals, to guide the church with and through the bishops as the successors to the apostles. He actually told them that it did not seem right to him, even as Pope, to give his blessings to his fellow apostles. Therefore, all the Cardinals together gave their blessings to each other and to the whole world at the close of the conclave.

The new Pope's intention of close consultation with the bishops in governing the Church will not mean great immediate changes in the Curia or in the dioceses and parishes throughout the world. But it will mean new and more charitable relationships between pastors and people as individuals and through parish councils once the new Pope's style of rule takes effect. His style will mean a reorganization of many church offices giving them a pastoral and human approach to the manifold challenges of our age.

The bishops will hear the call to get immediately involved with the poor in their slum dwellings and in the many blighted and threatened areas throughout their dioceses. Through John Paul II, the world's bishops will hear the echo of their call to first be pastors of the countless precious souls — rich and poor — entrusted to them by the Good Shepherd. To do this, they must tramp the streets of their dioceses as Christ tramped the roads of Palestine.

The Curia will also see considerable, wide scattered changes. Certainly new officials — cardinals, bishops, priests, nuns, and lay people — will take over many of the positions held by well-meaning but often isolated Vatican prelates.

No one expects an inundation of priests, nuns, clerics and lay people from Poland as happens after the election of a president or a governor in a secular political situation, although most probably the Polish Communist authorities would love to have such an exodus. But new blood and new ways for spreading the Gospel everywhere and the new appreciation for the expertise of the mass media — television, radio, journalism, artistic, and message-carrying forms of all types— can be expected from a Pope who once belonged to the "Rhapsodic Theatre" group in Poland, and from a man who knows the thrill of the ski trails, canoeing in the white rapid streams and calm lakes of his native land and of Italy, and who believes that God's creation took place in a great splurge of light and joy. As for the church's prayers, and its liturgical life, a wholly new impetus is to be expected, slowly but surely from a Pope who, as Cardinal, crowded into the basement of a church in Krakow and watched a performance of *Jesus Christ Super Star* by his non-professional, younger faithful.

Conservatives and progressives in the church have much to look forward to from John Paul II, a man who all his life survived by outmaneuvering the wily governors of his native Poland. He will surely know how to satisfy both the Catholics who want a strict law-and-order regimen in their church and their fellow Catholics seeking "The freedom of the Sons of God" preached by Christ in the Gospel.

Catholics who are still gravely worried about problems of responsible parenthood, parents who are concerned that their children do not go to church because "It doesn't do anything for them," and all Christians who feel discriminated against because of color, nationality, or poverty, can know that the new Holy Father shares their worries. They can be sure he will, with the prayers and aid of God's mother, the Lady of Czestochowa, as well as with the intelligence God gave him, do his best to find solutions.

The man who now rules the Church as the Bishop of Rome did not take the name of John Paul II without knowing very well what he would be up against in restoring unity within the Catholic Church itself before he could bring love of one's neighbor and love of one's enemy among Christians and then among all mankind. As he has just shouldered his awesome, yet sacred ministry, he has the hopes and prayers of millions around the world that their burdens might be a bit lighter because of this new man called Holy Father — a son from Poland.